To Patrick
to a treasured
colleague and friend.

Aydon.

What others are saying about *Trauma to Tango*

"Aydan Dunnigan's journey from the dark, sinister closet of his childhood takes him first into grim religion and then eventually into the sensuous, healing arms of the tango. Dunnigan's deeply personal, bone-honest memoir is a gift of grace and hope for all of us who suffer or have suffered. Simply put, it teaches us to dance."

Scott McKeen, Journalist, Media Consultant, Mental Health Advocate

"... completely captivating.... You write beautifully.... You earned this reader's trust and engagement through both the rhetorical reach of your writing and also through its honesty and wit...."

Jannie Edwards, Award-winning author of Blood Opera: The Raven Tango Poems

"Trauma to Tango is a rare and authentic account of one man's struggle and the process he went through to be healed. His raw honesty, internal conflicts between his faith, dreams and ideals are captivating as he struggles to be real to himself. The reader is able to accompany him in his journey as the dynamics of mental health, spirituality and psychotherapy play their role in catharsis."

Gavin Lam, MSW, BSW, RSW, Seminary Student

AYDAN DUNNIGAN M.DIV.

Trauma to Tango

Dancing Through the Shadows of Unforgiven Dreams

A Memoir

Dunnigan, Aydan

Trauma to Tango:
Dancing Through the Shadows of Unforgiven Dreams
A Memoir

Printed March 2013
Cover art by Lorraine Shulba
Design by PageMaster Publication Services

> 11434 120 Street
> Edmonton, AB T5G 2Y2
>
> 780.425.9303

Contact information: aydan.tango@gmail.com

> www.traumatotango.com

ISBN: 978-0-9866999-3-1

Published by: Earth Sky Reflections

> www.earthskyreflections.ca

Order online at www.traumatotango.com or
www.ShopPageMaster.ca

PUBLICATION ASSISTANCE AND
DIGITAL PRINTING IN CANADA BY

PageMaster
PUBLICATION SERVICES INC.
www.pagemaster.ca
780-425-9303

Let no one lightly set about such a work. Memory, once waked, will play the tyrant. I found I must set down...passions and thoughts of my own which I had clean forgotten. The past which I wrote down was not the past that I thought I had (all these years) been remembering. I did not, even when I had finished the book, see clearly many things that I see now. The change which the writing wrought in me (and of which I did not write) was only a beginning – only to prepare me for the gods' surgery. They used my own pen to probe my wound.

C.S. Lewis, *Till We Have Faces.*

We set up for ourselves in the first dozen years of our life all of the stumbling blocks or traumas we will need for our growth, balance or eventual wholeness and then spend 30-40 years re-working these themes until at last we rejoin our essence in beauty and fullness.

Gwendolyn Jansma PhD, *Letters*

CONTENTS

PREFACE

Deep in the dense wood of the subconscious
cower chunks of my childhood,
memories that surface only as searing pain.

For most of my life I successfully kept them suppressed in the dark.
At mid-life, in the midst of my bid for respectability and stability
as a Protestant pastor and devoted father,
these memories began to seep back into my conscious awareness.
A frail, haunting voice called out from deep within,
at first inviting but then demanding attention.
At night I would be visited by nightmares.
During the day I would be overcome by body tremors
which would send me doubled over a toilet bowl.

In the end I could ignore the voice no longer and began the journey inward,
down the long road to the dark forest to seek
out the source of these torments.
Not because I wanted to.
I was compelled to.

With each step I struggled against
shadows of shame and recrimination that shrouded my path,
whispering that I deserved or even invited the lewd attention.
A curtain of judgement, fashioned in those moments of abuse and betrayal,
choked out my sense of power and pride.
A cloak of religious piety, clinging like a spider's web,
condemned my soul as wicked and my body flawed,
numbing me to nurturing touch and intimacy.

Still the voice called.
Through the deadening layers of self-doubt and mistrust I pressed on,
ever closer to the secrets that could not be named,
inspired by the sympathetic image of a delicate, disfigured child,
in need of my love and protection.

As I entered the heart of the forest, the last veil parted.
There he sat, not the crippled child that I had envisioned
but a child of brilliant light, intense pure energy and beauty.
"I have been waiting for you," he said. "I have kept myself
protected in the deep wood until you were strong enough and wise
and courageous enough to make this journey. You have earned
the right to claim my brilliant beauty as part of your soul."
He reached out with strong but tender hands, "Take me home."
I opened my arms and heart and welcomed
his embrace into my mine.
Orphans no longer.

Thus the journey ends and begins.

INTRODUCTION

Memoirs and autobiographies are forms of fiction, because memory is fiction. By the time you remember something, you're already telling a story.

Douglas Barbour, Westword, Nov 2012.

After half a life of unsuccessful attempts to cleanse and sanctify his past, the author abandons his spiritual quest to right childhood wrongs and sinks back into a world of shadows. From these same shadows emerges the dance of tango weaving together conflicting strands of tragedy and beauty, the earthy and ethereal. Born in the brothels and bordellos of Buenos Aires and crafted on the blood soaked floors of slaughterhouses, tango embodies the human spirit's indomitable thirst for romance, artistry and elegance.

At first blush, it might appear rather brash and insensitive to consider childhood trauma and sexual abuse in conjunction with dance, especially tango with its overtures of the sensual and erotic. Nonetheless, I was directed in my journey by the conviction that I could heal inner wounds through integrating and enacting those disparate dynamics on the dance floor.

As a young child, in order to mitigate the pain of trauma, I had become skilled at *dissociating* - the art of disconnecting body from spirit. I could capably convince myself during the abuse that I was *somewhere* else or *someone* else. I *absented* my body and numbed myself to sensory stimuli and awareness. With the further encouragement of religion I learned to mistrust my instinctual self and distance myself from the sensual and sexual.

By mid-life my strategy of repression and denial was unravelling, the causalities including a divorce and a forced exit from the ordained pastorate. The time had come to reintegrate myself as a full-bodied and full-spirited human.

Enter tango (following closely on the heels of a newfound loving relationship). Through its signature chest-to-chest embrace, the distinctively different step patterns for the lead and follow, and its extemporaneous non-choreographed flow, tango brings to the dance floor all the relational dynamics and communication patterns that one experiences in real-life relationships. It requires acute sensitivity to the positioning, responsiveness and abilities of one's partner and the willingness of both to blend expectations and movement in sculpting a fluid dance.

This was not an easy adaptation. Initially as a *50-something* dance student, I was incapable of translating and modelling the teacher's instruction. It was as if everything were in an indecipherable code (the residue of *dissociation*). Fortunately, dance is precisely the anti-dote to this type of deficit, With time and repetition it develops communication between mind and body on a sensual and visceral level.

But tango goes even deeper. It touched on wounds left from childhood imprinting, where I learned that intimacy and vulnerability were opportunities for abuse. By bringing these issues directly onto the dance floor and immersing myself in the intimacy of the moment, I empowered my body to resolve the turmoil and confusion created by this early scripting. I began to trust my sexuality and sensuality that I had previously feared and despised. I absorbed into my muscular fibre all the expansiveness and passion needed for love and relationships.

The journey then, which began in darkness and fear, has expanded into transformation. It is much more than simply undoing ancient wrongs. I move forward not as a recovering victim but as an inspired artist who embraces the breadth of pathos and passion as part of the dance, channelling the polar energies into something of grace and beauty.

The gift to this unending process of discovering and uncovering extends far beyond the dance floor. It empowers me to revisit the normal warp and woof of life with an increased capacity for love and joy. The tragedy and pain extracted from my past and amplified through dance, expands my personal boundaries and makes it possible for my spirit to embrace the polarities with compassion.

Through this layered antiphony of reflection and movement, I sort through the ecstatic and salient episodes, the love and abuse, joy and pain that have shaped my life to this point. The exercise becomes an interplay between woundedness, duplicity and confusion and the redemptive forces in my life, sometimes as an expression of hope, stumbling blindly into the future, sometimes as a search for meaning, tracing my steps back through memories of abuse and abandonment, successes and failures. An invitation is extended from *Source* to embrace it all as *gift*, drawing together with grace and forgiveness that which reveals something of the dance of life and the joy of being alive.

MONSTER IN THE BEDROOM

One or two things are all you need to travel over the blue pond...
some deep memory of pleasure, some cutting knowledge of pain....

Mary Oliver, *New and Selected Poems.*

Growing up on the North Shore of Lake Superior, a child learns to embrace life through the pores of the skin.

My childhood buddy Scott and I careen across the iced expanse of the largest skating rink in the world. Ours. The steel wind drives us forward, skate blades scoring the marbled ice, frozen hands gripping the bed sheet billowing between us. Shards of crystallized air lacerate our face and lungs. No thought is given to the exhausting skate home.

The tentacled rays of the morning summer sun seep in through my bedroom window, prying lose my survival-grip on my teddy bear, guardian of the night. First up and out, I step into the back yard and am assaulted by a barrage of smells and sounds: buzzing bees and trilling robins and scents of lilac and apple blossoms wafting on a bracing breeze. In the distance is the hypnotic cadence of waves washing over the rocky shoreline, unrelenting in the primal motion of cleansing, sculpting and polishing.

My girl-friend Sandy and I follow the well-worn path across

the field behind the house and climb to the top of the hill. From there, so it seems, one can see beyond the earth's curvature. We sink down into the welcoming grass, warmth radiating up from the granite rock of the Pre-Cambrian Shield. A cooling breeze blows gently off Lake Superior. A solitary freighter creeping out from behind the Sleeping Giant threads its way across the horizon, a pencil line of smoke tracing its passage. Clouds drift overhead in fanciful shapes, sunlight dances hypnotically off the water. Our fantasies carry us away to a world of our creating, a world without pain and abuse. Sandy envisions herself a ballerina, spinning freely, I a kite, soaring ever higher until home diminishes to a pinpoint below.

Our stately childhood home stood on an acre of highway frontage, serving as a prop for the distinguished community profile that my parents had cultivated. Inside, the main floor was open concept, with the den, dining room and living room blended into one large area. There was hardwood floor throughout and a large granite and amethyst fireplace at the far end, a focal point for parties that went on into the wee hours of the morning.

What provided extra space on the main floor created congestion on the second. All five siblings were squeezed into two bedrooms. My sister got a room all to herself. We four boys, spanning an age range of over ten years, co-habited the other room.

A bedroom is an intimate environment where much more gets shared than simply dressers and bunk beds. It is the stage for life's most formative experiences and exchanges, a place of vulnerability and intimacy. Often a blanket pulled tightly over the head is the only protection against disturbing intrusions from a sordid adult world. Often it is not enough.

Sandy is sleeping over, she in the upper bunk, I on the bottom. The adults are downstairs, thick into their partying. The sound of footsteps ascending the staircase are barely perceptible above the din. A bulky frame stands silhouetted in the bedroom doorway and then enters the room. The ladder strains at the end of the bed. The pleas, muffled protests, whimpers, sobs are swallowed by the darkness.

I lay motionless in the bed beneath, under the covers, clinging to my teddy bear.

In a recurring nightmare, I am sitting on a stool, alone in the middle of a cold, damp basement. In the shadows stirs a large, grotesque, toad-like creature. It rouses itself and begins heading in my direction. I try desperately to escape but am frozen to this stool, paralysed. The monster emerges from the shadows. A low, throbbing pulse vibrates in the floorboards and rafters. I try to run but am not able to escape. On reaching me, it swallows me whole, and then regurgitates me and spits me out. I am returned to the stool, inside out, a slimy, marbled, jelly-textured blob.

I wet my bed, again.

On my fifth birthday I receive my favourite gift of all time: a 78 LP, *Howdy Doody and the Musical Forest*.

"Hello boys and girls. My name is Buffalo Bob Smith and I'm here to tell you about an amazing adventure of my friend Howdy Doody."

And what an amazing adventure it is. I clamber up into the back of the piano with Howdy and Twinkle, the good musical elf, and journey to the Good Musical Forest. At the same time, in another part of town Mr. Bluster slides down his big bass tuba with

Clunky, the mean musical elf, and they exit into the Mean Musical Forest where all the bad musical sounds are made.

Eventually Howdy and Mr. Bluster, Twinkle and Clunky all end up in the same woods on that fateful morning when the Good Musical Forest and the Bad Musical Forest determine to settle their differences by going to war. At the height of the battle, with the two opposing musical forests hurtling music at the other side with all the might they can muster, Howdy rushes into the thick of the conflict. Through his courage and impertinence he convinces the warring factions to become friends and play together in harmony.

Howdy Doody was my spiritual mentor, a puppet of courage and principle, always ready to say and do the right thing. Of course he had his detractors, like Mister Bluster, who was as lacking in moral fibre as much as Howdy was exuding it. But despite his geeky clothes and freckled face, Howdy was able to overcome obstacles, overpower bullies and make the world a kinder place.

I determine that when my chance to confront evil comes, I will rush into the middle of the conflict and get everyone to shake hands and be friends, just like Howdy.

On my sister's dresser was a small, ornate ivory, white and pink music box with a soldier and ballerina dancing to the intricacies of a Mozart sonata. Sandy and I would steal it away into the closet down the hall and allow ourselves to be enfolded within its magic. The young soldier, outfitted in a red Victorian Infantry uniform with gold buttons and buckles and shoulder hasps, would assume his supportive role gallantly. His prima ballerina, laced in white from head to toe, would pirouette on the rotating pedestal. Her one arm was raised overhead and her other rested on the shoulder of her protector as she balanced gracefully on one foot. For hours the two would circle each other delicately, tirelessly, hypnotically.

But today the enchantment is broken. Footfalls interrupt from down the hallway. The creaking door cuts through the tinkling melody. The monster presses. The music box is knocked aside. The soldier snaps from his post on the pedestal and tumbles into the shadows. His ballerina teeters and then falls into the arms of her abuser.

At some point in the throes of these unholy invasions, I begin to develop adaptive strategies: dissociation, blackouts, memory loss. My mind begins to lie about what is happening. My body stops feeling. My spirit leaves my body. I imagine myself to be somewhere else, pretending that I am not in danger and that this isn't happening to me.

At age seven, I went to see the Walt Disney movie *Bambi*. Here was nature at its most benign and romantic with swaying willows, chirping birds, soft cuddly animals that frolic through the wilderness without a care. All the while, Bambi is safe and secure as the sole object of his mother's affection.

Then the unthinkable happens. The pristine, pastoral setting is rent asunder by the violent intrusion of some dark force. Fires flare and guns blast and quails scatter. Crows screech as frothing hunting dogs tear through the forest, viciously ripping apart everything in their path. Bambi's mother urges Bambi to run and hide. Bambi looks up in terror and bewilderment. "What's the matter, Mother?" His mother responds, "Man has entered the forest."

They begin their frenzied race through the woods, trying to outrun the fire and the dogs and the guns until, suddenly, a shot rings out and Bambi's mother falls. Bambi wanders aimlessly through the forest, crying, "Mother, where are you, Mother?"

Herein is revealed the deep secret of evil in the world. Men leave in their wake carnage and destruction and death. They destroy the innocence and safety of a child's world, leaving him scarred and alone. I for one, would defy the laws of my physiology and refuse to grow up to be a man and remain close to my mother for the rest of my life.

A recurring nightmare suggests otherwise: I go out behind the house among the spruce trees to pet a young fawn. It is sweet and soft and I am gentle and compassionate. Suddenly my fawn shape-shifts into a wolf, standing upright, fully clothed, talking. I am terrified by the wolf's cleverness and importunity and attempt to dream it back into the harmless fawn. It will not change. The door is fixed open onto an adult world marred by the conflicting realities of power and vulnerability, cunning and innocence, predator and prey.

⚜ TANGO INTERLUDE

I am not sure what delusions possessed my wife Patricia and I to sign up for tango lessons. Certainly, neither Patricia nor I anticipated the life-altering implications that committing to simple dance lessons would have.

We were celebrating our engagement at *La Boheme*, a romantic Heritage Inn in the distinguished Highlands neighbourhood of Edmonton, Alberta. After passing the night in the Da Vinci room, decorated in nineteenth century European décor, we rose the next morning to come down for breakfast. At the bottom of the broad ornate staircase was posted a picture of an attractive young woman seductively draped in a silky dress, clinging to her dashing partner. Tango lessons, Tuesday evening, at this very establishment. We signed up immediately.

What was the lure? Did we envision ourselves transformed into the slinky, sexy couple on the brochure? Perhaps we were in the mood to do something impetuous and risqué. Patricia and I rarely danced and our bodies were far beyond the slinky stage. Perhaps the raw sensuality and passion reawakened primal instincts that had been repressed or demonized.

Whatever the reason, our early lessons were nothing as advertized. Our attempts at tango were neither pretty nor the least bit erotic. It felt more like a stylized version of *all-star wrestling*. To translate what was being instructed and demonstrated into actual movements was excruciatingly painful for both of us. I would often just stare blankly at my feet, physically and mentally paralyzed, unable to discern my left from my right, let alone command them to move in a particular pattern. We would come away from our lessons sweating, frustrated, despairing that we would ever capture that romantic feeling that had first inspired our journey. Every once in a while, Patricia and I would catch a wave of symmetry. But mostly we persevered.

On a drive home from one of our frustrating lessons Patricia and I listen to a CBC radio documentary about Claude Debussy who, when he was young, was chided by his teachers for not following the prescribed form or technique. He pronounced boldly in defiance, "There are no rules. There is only pleasure."

I look over to Patricia. She responds with a knowing smile. *Pleasure* we can do.

AT THE CROSSROADS

I went down to the crossroads, fell down on my knees
I asked the Lord for mercy, save me if you please.

The Cream, *Crossroads*

Once I answered Yes to Someone - or Something. And from
that hour on I was certain that existence is meaningful and
that, therefore, my life, in self-surrender, has a goal.

Dag Hammorskjold, *Markings.*

The 60s were a turbulent time for everyone. This was the age of social reform, causes, protests, expecting that one's life would count for something. There was also the generation gap, the challenge to question authority and distance oneself from traditional family values. This allowed me the opportunity to create some separation between myself and the family dynamics that were so painful and problematic.

Armed with a strident adolescent spirit bracketed by a black-and-white world of moral absolutes, I embraced the vision of fashioning a different world, one with justice and honesty where big people didn't do bad things to children.

The classic 60's response to problems was to drop out and smoke up. I went from an A student to a D student and envisioned exiting from my last year of high school. Scott and I spent afternoons hanging out with the bums down by the railway tracks, practising being *anti-establishment.*

But none of these alternatives ever really got any traction as a viable lifestyle option. I did take my friends to my little log trapper's cabin, à la Thoreau and *On Walden Pond*, but they lacked my enthusiasm for living in a mosquito-infested bog, miles back in the bush. (Thoreau showed better judgement in situating his cabin on a pristine lake about a mile from town: he got company. Even so, he only lasted a little over a year in his handcrafted paradise.)

I made another pass at the same concept by fashioning a small geodesic dome and transporting it to a lake, with the intent of building my own little hermitage. Fortunately, some hunters made good use of it as firewood before we had chance to complete the assembling. It saved me further disillusionment.

It didn't take much insight to figure out that a broader, more inclusive foundation for the global village was needed. Being cool and doing drugs was hardly an adequate basis for transforming society. The Beatles gave it their best shot with Transcendental Meditation and "All you need is Love." Dylan gave potent expression to the anger and alienation. But all that wore thin eventually. The Beatles broke up in a very unloving fashion. Dylan went country. Jim and Jimi and Janis OD'd.

I was left stranded, frantically searching for something to address the moral confusion and uncertainties, within and without. An identity crisis dogged me: Who am I? Where do I fit in? What will I do with my life? Having outgrown Howdy Doody, I was in need of a new hero, a role model. Who then? Mick Jagger? Alan Ginsberg? My father? My brother? A more comprehensive strategy was needed for correcting the deficiencies and dysfunction of my childhood.

Jesus Freaks to the rescue! For me and a generation of seekers, this was the perfect answer: a total makeover for Christianity so that it actually looked like *new wave*, rather than the spent force of my parent's generation. Jesus became the new counter-cultural hero, voted *Man of the Year* by *Time Magazine* (how astute of them).

He was now an anti-establishment, long-haired radical, a friend of the street folk and enemy of those in power.

Being a Jesus freak offered the perfect moral vantage point from which to true my spiritual compass. It had been stuck between finding guilty those whom I idealized (the big powerful people in my family), and blaming the innocent victims, in this case Sandy and me. Enter Jesus, who commanded me to forgive everyone: "Let he who is without sin cast the first stone." I could forgive, forget and reframe everything of my prior existence, as if the old wounds and grief had never existed.

With the anthem from Cream reverberating in the background, I headed *down to the crossroads* in a courageous attempt to reset my life's course.

Summer Solstice, June 21, 1969. A day before my 16th birthday. A lazy summer afternoon. But I was restless, agitated. There was something churning inside, a question demanding attention. I had no idea what it was, but I became obsessed with finding an answer nonetheless. Impulsively, I dusted off my father's King James Version Masonic Bible (his principal contribution to my religious orientation) with the sayings of Jesus highlighted in red ink:

> Except a man be born again he cannot enter the kingdom of
> Heaven... What does it profit to gain the whole world but lose one's
> soul? ...Come unto me all ye who labour and I will give you rest.

The appeals, the invitations, the blessings and curses, hopes and promises were all there in bold red letters. Jesus was asking me to make a calculated, life-changing decision: to weigh out the pros and cons of a life lived with God or without God. I had no idea how involved a procedure having one's soul *saved* was or how successful I could hope to be. Nonetheless, I would give it most serious consideration. The bold red print made it clear that this was an all-or-nothing proposition.

Off I trounced to my safe place in the woods, with a sleeping bag and a straw hat, a bit of food and my newly acquired red-letter King James Version Masonic Bible. There was a beautiful hill overlooking our favourite fishing hole about four miles down the road, a long ambling bend in the McGregor River with the railway running alongside. This would certainly allow a proper, expansive vista for reflection, alone with the birds, frogs and mosquitoes. Nothing to distract me (except for the mosquitoes). No one to embarrass me while I prayed.

The entire day was spent walking up and down the train tracks alongside the river, challenging the silence of the universe, searching the sky for an awareness of some presence. My prayers and pleas refracted lamely off the clouds. I was all alone, not so much as a train to challenge my wandering and chase me off the tracks. Strange that in such a beautiful natural setting I could not find the enchantment that Wordsworth or Emerson or Thoreau wrote about. There was something missing. My pristine solitude seemingly could not address the emptiness within.

The day wore on and I was no closer to finding my answer. At sunset I found a spot out by the river to bed down for the night, pulled my hat down over my head to ward off the mosquitoes, and set to sleep, serenaded by a cacophony of birds and frogs arranging their worlds before the settling darkness.

I awoke in the morning without so much as a dream in response to my searching. *On to Plan B.* I would go to the Baptist church that we used to attend as a family years prior. I rolled up my bag, grabbed my hat and walked back home. My mother was there for me, as always, and offered to drive me into town. I didn't bother changing and continued my journey in ratty jeans and a T-shirt, reeking of McCurdy's fly repellent.

Up the front steps of First Baptist Church I plodded to the massive oak doors defying the assaults of the modern world. I pulled on the brass handles. Inside was dark and empty as a tomb.

I entered the sanctuary and slid inconspicuously into a pew half-way down the aisle, unnoticed by everyone except the 20-foot tall stained-glass Jesus. There he was, just as I had left him several years ago, knocking on the door of someone's heart. Today it was mine.

The sermon that day, like the sermons most days, called on the *lost* to *give their heart to Jesus*. It ended with the minister coming down in front and giving an old-fashioned altar call: "Is there anyone who wants to dedicate their life to Jesus?" The congregation was singing a gospel hymn just like in the Billy Graham crusades, which went on and on forever to ensure that everyone had the opportunity to respond to the call.

I lasted four verses of the hymn but then broke rank and ventured out from my pew. More correctly, I was pried loose. At that moment my feet did not belong to me and my mind and body were on auto-pilot. I stumbled down to the front and wandered around somewhat aimlessly, dazed, bewildered. I was really not clear where I was or what was going on. One of the choir members kindly directed me into the minister's study, and I stayed there until the minister came in and we prayed together. Not that I knew much about praying. Nonetheless, his comment after was that it was the most spirit-filled prayer that he had ever experienced. I remember little or nothing, other than crying for much of the afternoon.

So there it was: converted in old-fashioned gospel style, filled with the Holy Spirit, born again as a disciple of Jesus. Something had changed for me that day, proving that when the heart is opened in egoless vulnerability, thirsting for love and meaning, the *storehouses of heaven* are indeed opened and the Universe responds with gentle nurture.

THE STRAIGHT AND NARROW

If a man does not keep pace with his companions,
perhaps it is because he marches to the beat of a different drummer.
Let him step to the music which he hears, however measured or far away.

Henry David Thoreau

Perhaps it was all too good to be true, a bit of a set-up. When I saw the twenty-foot stained-glass Jesus standing with his arms outstretched, welcoming, accepting, forgiving, I leapt headlong. To a shame-ridden, insecure adolescent, it looked like a safe place of solace, if there ever was one.

Yet somehow in the middle of my leap of faith, the trajectory got slightly skewed. My landing wasn't nearly as soft and comforting as I had expected. What happened to all that promised unconditional love and acceptance? How was it that I ended with more guilt and shame than before?

Apparently one's status as a beloved child of God is somewhat tenuous; all the comforting assurances that the large red print giveth, the small black print taketh away. It is one thing to *get saved*; it's another thing to *stay saved*. One can go through all the effort of getting one's name written in the Book of Life only to have it erased by committing the *unpardonable sin* (whatever that was). One has to keep on one's guard at all times, protecting one's soul against the sins of the flesh and the wiles of the Devil. Scary business.

The essential problem, according to fundamentalist Christianity, is that the human spirit is in conflict with Divine Spirit, simply by virtue of being human. I was deeply flawed; everything about me was sinful and deceitful (as was the rest of the natural order).

What was required to keep me saved was a denial or repression of my humanity. There was no room in the life of the devout for a personal agenda, natural inclinations, and instinctual feelings. Being a follower of Jesus required diligent training and discipline, elevating mind and will over body and emotions.

This teaching readily fostered self-loathing and self-abuse. A penchant for masochism came in very handy. Gothic novels about missionaries and martyrs were the order of the day: people who gave up wealth, fame, social standing, even their life, to proclaim the gospel. One of our required readings in seminary was *Fox's Book of Martyrs*, which chronicled gruesome descriptions of saints experiencing every manner of torture and mutilation in exchange for eternal salvation. Saint Paul was executed. Saint Stephen was stoned. Saint Peter hung upside down on the cross. Getting speared by Indians in the jungles of the Amazon and roasted over an open-pit fire, (a more contemporary example), could be considered a very noble aspiration. The general gist was that if you managed to somehow manoeuvre through life without at least losing a limb or an essential bodily function, you weren't trying hard enough.

In this modern world, one might look a little askance at this *kamikaze* approach to faith. Living with a death-wish is generally viewed as not a particularly healthy mindset. However, I was swimming in a stream of Christianity that honoured suffering and ignominious death as the highest expression of one's love for God, in the same way that Jesus' suffering on the cross was in some peculiar way an expression of Divine love.

This equation had the effect of inextricably linking pain with passion, relationship with suffering, intimacy with violence. My childhood experience fitted into this paradigm with precision, intimacy and perversity being flip sides of the same coin. All this self-abuse to get a little affection or attention seemed like a fair deal to me.

Whatever it took, I was up for the challenge, quite prepared to sacrifice my dignity and self-respect if it would get me closer to God. Seeking public ridicule and scorn became my version of flagellation. Where it was not readily to be found, I became very creative in manufacturing it, sacrificing the few social graces that I had acquired to this higher calling. I humiliated myself in whatever way imaginable for Jesus' sake, parading my faith with a sandwich board draped over my shoulders, witnessing door to door and bus stop to bus stop, cornering unsuspecting fellow transit users and urging them to give their lives to Jesus. I spoke at conferences, preached on street-corners, arm-twisted my peers. My answer was now the world's answer. I was in evangelistic attack mode!

For a few idealistic years I successfully modelled this committed discipleship lifestyle. I attended every Bible Study and church service, responded to every altar call, lined up every time someone was offering a fresh dose of the Holy Spirit. In good Freudian fashion, natural instincts and attractions were repressed or channelled into religious fanaticism. Surely this was a foolproof system to correct all that was defective, elevate me to moral purity and choke out the last blood-drop of fallen humanity. Whatever it would take to purge myself of myself.

Although it is easy to parody this stage of life, it was in many respects a courageous response to the ambiguities within. It provided a sense of direction and purpose that I would have lacked otherwise and soothed my *existential angst* (very big on campus at the time). And it served as an inspiration for more than a few others. Even my university professors, whom I relentlessly harassed, would complement me at the end of the term for my earnestness. There was certainly no denying that I was earnest.

But there was something more substantive evolving, a knitting together in my spirit of an appreciation for truth and beauty and transcendence. It was the fashioning of that soul for which I had been searching, that part of the Self that chooses the higher moral ground even at personal expense, and draws one relentlessly toward life and love. Howdy would have been proud.

THE HALO FADES

It is better to marry than to burn in lust.

Saint Paul

Raging adolescent hormones were pressing from behind. In front was the terrifying prospect of repeating the offences that had been visited on my friend and me.

First on the spiritual agenda was to put to bed (metaphorically speaking) the demon sex. Jesus issued the caution:

> If thy eye offend thee pluck it out or if your hand offend thee, cut it off. It is better for thee to enter into life … maimed, rather than having two hands or two feet to be cast into everlasting fire.

Sure, the passage didn't refer directly to sex, but any adolescent male knew what sins involving hands and eyes was referring to.

As a biblical literalist, I was forced to do some serious calculations. The prospects didn't look good. My socialization in matters of sexuality ranged from misogyny to rape. There had been no modelling of respect for boundaries, relational intimacy, or nonviolent sexuality. Everything played into a dominance/ submission model with someone getting damaged along the way. Marriage seemingly was my only refuge from causing serious harm to myself or someone else. I could marry and have sex, in that order, and I was not to enjoy either.

My strategy then in marriage, was to find someone with whom I had little in common, commit myself to an untenable relationship and make it work out of sheer strength of will – another ill-advised attempt at driving a wedge between body and spirit, passion and piety. A mitigating factor against forming a healthy, loving, adult relationship (generally considered to be the foundation of marriage), was that I retained the subconscious conviction that caring for someone would be the occasion for their getting hurt (imprinting from the bunk-bed travesty). It would be safer, according to my traumatized childhood illogic, to not get emotionally attached at all. To do otherwise would be to put both myself and the one for whom I cared at risk.

Off I went in search of an unsuspecting marriage partner with whom I would share my entire life with the exception of my heart. As divine providence would have it, I found Beth, quiet, mild-mannered, unassuming, who didn't require that I make much of an emotional investment in our relationship. Perfect match.

Another item on my shopping list for the ideal spouse was someone who would support me in my chosen path of sainthood, with stops along the way of becoming a Baptist minister and then a missionary and then a martyr. Beth had grown up in a pastor's family, had a much better sense of social propriety than I did (most everyone did), and presumably knew what it would take to manage a ministerial household. I could also learn some normal human virtues like courtesy and consideration. This marriage could serve as a very useful training, a sort of basic civility boot camp.

What I didn't factor in was that Beth was of a different denomination with different ambitions and no intention whatsoever of following me into a Baptist church, let alone the ministry or the jungles of Borneo. Her father was a Missouri Synod Lutheran minister and a particularly strict one out of a particularly severe lot. This shouldn't seem like much of an issue in this modern broad-minded society, but that did not describe either of the worlds that we came from. I believed that anyone other than a born-again fundamentalist was damned to hell, and Beth's father, who did most of the believing for their family, felt the same about me. For whatever reason, Beth and I weren't able to anticipate that this would result in marital conflict.

Then there was conflict over social values. Beth was a middle-class woman with no real interest in renouncing material pleasures or joining a commune, which was all the rage at the time. I think she actually had the notion of creating a normal life with normal comforts and enjoyments. I should have heeded St. Paul's cautions against marriage and cut off my genitals when it was still an option. Now the only choices were adapt or divorce. (This was long before win-win solutions were conceived.)

Adapt I did. The cracks in my Jesus Freak facade began to widen. It was becoming increasingly unlikely that I would ever be shot by savages or tied to a stake on a man-eating ant hill. Instead I would be condemned to live a fairly normal life of only average virtue.

My only recourse was to make the sacrament of marriage a spiritual ordeal. I could submit to all these modern conveniences like matching living-room furniture and a toaster oven and 15" colour TV, as long as I remembered to suffer them with indignation. As for sex, I would indulge my partner her conjugal rights but strictly out of a sense of duty and self-sacrifice. (Sure I enjoyed myself plenty, but I didn't have to admit it.)

Strange as it seems, I did not come up with this ascetic, antiseptic notion of love and marriage myself. In addition to St. Paul's misogynistic counsel, there were very respectable contemporary advocates of the painful, passionless life. C.S. Lewis wrote a Christian classic, *The Four Loves*, in which he suggested that true love was an exercise of self-sacrifice, detachment and obedience, and weakened by feelings and self-interest. There was no recognition of the elements we normally attribute to a healthy relationship, such as affection, sharing thoughts and feelings, caring, acceptance, empathy, touching, listening, giving, respecting, helping, appreciating, supporting, etc. This love is a mental construct sustained by sheer strength of will!

The symbiosis between my inner woundedness and religiosity was now firmly entrenched. Religion became my survival strategy, charting a moral high ground and reigning in impulse-driven adolescent instincts (of the *little head vs. big head* variety). As a young man standing at the edge of the daunting, complex, compromised world of adulthood, this commitment to a life of faith seemed like the safest and most secure refuge from the shame of a scarred youth. My religious beliefs allowed me to mask or assuage my troubled psyche without confronting the source of the pain, with dismissives such as "It's God's will," or "Forgive and forget." My born-again conversion experience segregated me from earlier life experiences, excusing me from attending to any antecedents: "The old has passed away. All things have become new," in the words of the Good Book.

I was mistaken. The old continued to haunt and hamstring. The roots of my spiritual life remained melded with those messy bits from that vulnerable and impressionable period of my life, effectively redirecting the energy required for healing into fundamentalist fervour. As it turned out, when childhood demons came to call, religion and the church were the most dangerous places of all to be.

❧ TANGO INTERLUDE

Our first tango teachers, Ernst and Tamara, owners of La Boheme, embodied the flare for drama and passion that exemplified tango. Tamara, a perfectly postured beautiful young woman, brought her perfectionist tendencies to everything from her dancing to her photography. Ernst, a professional dancer in his earlier life, inspired me with his sense of bodily presence, moving with confidence and grace and self-awareness. He would try to put this into words – "be here in this space, not in front or behind you and walk as if there is a string tying you to the ceiling" – making as much sense as my yoga teacher telling me to breathe through the soles of my feet and exhale through my navel.

In our first lesson we are taught the proper posture for dancing, which involves squaring up the upper frame of your body with your partner. This is critical. Stand erect. Chest out, stomach in. The woman senses the lead through the subtle movement of the man's chest and responds by repositioning her chest in front of his.

The drama and tension of the dance is developed when the man moves his chest out of alignment, either by turning or stepping away. The woman's chest must now go searching for him. To do so, she steps around the man which, if done in good form, creates a tango step. The man may attempt to thwart the woman's attempt at chest alignment by disrupting the woman's walking, with an intrusive foot placement or by stepping off in another direction. There are moments where they come together, but only momentarily, before the man again disrupts the alignment and the chase begins again with renewed vigour.

All this talk about chests makes me somewhat light-headed. I look around the room. There are some very pronounced specimens. How will I feel about lining up with them? In such a predicament, I do the only thing a respectable gentleman can do – I cave. My shoulders slouch and my chest collapses. In the words of our bio-energetics instructor, I hide my power.

Ernst detects the hesitancy and leads us in a pronounced prance around the room. For fifteen minutes every class we practice this posture, chest out, head back, strutting about with presence and assertiveness like young cocks in a hen house.

ON THE ROAD

Certainly those determining acts of her life were not ideally beautiful.
They were the mixed result of young and noble impulse struggling amidst
the conditions of an imperfect social state, in which great feelings will
often take the aspect of error, and great faith the aspect of illusion.

George Eliot, *Middlemarch*.

Ten years, 10,000 miles and $10,000 later (education was cheaper in those days), Beth and I were still working out a compromise to our religious differences. From one coast to the other and back again, through twelve moves and three theological colleges, I remained determined to go into the ministry. Beth was determined that it not be the Baptist ministry.

I had committed myself to the notion that "all things work for good," *(The Good Book)*. If this was the *good*, I didn't want to see the *bad*. There were some very serious problems developing, not the least being that I was not the model of perfection that I had believed I would be. Nor was my marriage. My life was not unfolding according to script.

We spent the first year of our marriage and almost our last at a Baptist Seminary in the Annapolis Valley, Nova Scotia. Beth made it clear at that point that if we did not return home together, she was quite prepared to return without me. Getting a divorce at this stage of my studies would effectively *kibosh* any future in the Baptist ministry, so again I caved.

Our denominational tug-of-war continued for the next ten years, touching down briefly at a non-denominational college in Vancouver and then settling at Lutheran Theological Seminary in

Saskatchewan. Eventually we made it to that very special day when I became ordained as a Lutheran minister.

Despite my initial reservations, I snuggled in tightly for the long haul with no thought of breaking out. I took a solemn vow before the congregation, the communion of saints, God and the angels that I would forever think, believe, and act in keeping with the defined tenets of the Lutheran Church. Let them bury me in this straightjacket.

Ordination is a very peculiar composite of social and spiritual energies that wraps up one's whole being like a cocoon: restricting, comforting, protecting. It is a contract or covenant between the church and the cleric, exchanging autonomy and independence for security and social function: you be there for Mother Church and Mother Church will be there for you. Material security, vocation, social standing, public persona are knit together with faith, beliefs and values. It was the *full-meal deal*, an *all-or-nothing* package, growing old as an *adult child* suckled at the breast of Mother Church.

I welcomed this. For the time being all my uncertainties and anxieties were resolved. I belonged. Ordination answered all the searching questions about who I was, what was I to do with my life and what God and others expected of me. Most importantly, I had a new family, Jesus my brother, God my Heavenly Father.

Although I had yet to cultivate an affinity for Lutheranism, by this stage of the game I seceded to the compromise, still resolved to climb back up on a pedestal (read: pulpit). Better a Lutheran pastor than none at all.

With a measure of misgiving, I swallowed the pill. And a bitter pill it was: very bleak business, this Lutheranism. The bumper sticker, *Life is hard and then you die*, was no doubt adapted from the Lutheran liturgy:

> I, a poor, miserable sinner, confess to Thee all my sins and iniquities with which I have ever offended Thee and justly deserve Thy punishment now and forever. But I am heartily sorry for them and sincerely repent of them,

and I pray Thee … to be gracious and merciful to me, a poor sinful being.

One gets the picture very early in the Sunday service that this is not *happy hour.*

Lutheran theology trashed the perfectionist view that I had as a Baptist, namely, that I should strive to be a better person and that I should expect to make significant progress in this regard. With Lutheranism, there is no such expectation. Whatever improvements I think I might be making, under the scrutiny of God's absolutist standards they really don't amount to much more than self-delusion. I am judged, not so much for the *guilt of mal-doing* but the *shame of mal-being.* Fortunately God happens to be in the business of loving the unloveable and forgiving the unpardonable. When I confess my unworthiness I am, in God's eyes, absolved of all my failings and shortcomings.

The intriguing aspect of this disparaging view of my human condition was that it did suggest some comfort. I shared the conviction that I was deeply flawed and fractured at a soul level and warranted divine censorship (although *temporal and eternal punishment* might have been overstating it somewhat). As a child, I was unable to create an healthy ego-boundary for myself and as a consequence internalized the psychological states of *abused, abuser, and rescuer.* I presumed that I caused the abuse, or invited it, or at least in some fashion should have been able to prevent it.

Two of these orientations, rescuer and victim, fit in well with my religious faith. The *victim mentality,* with it a sense of powerlessness, shame, assumed guilt and perforated boundaries, lent itself readily to the abdication of personal power and judgement to the unquestionable teachings of the Bible and the Church. My *rescuer mindset* supported my idealist charge as *defender of the faith and protector of the weak and needy.* The real problem was, "What to do with the monster's predatory instincts which construed vulnerability and intimacy into an opportunity for dominance and abuse?" *Lest I do unto others as had been done unto me,* I subjected myself to rigorous repression of sensuality and passion. I immersed myself in disciplines of prayer and biblical studies and took vows of ordination and marriage to curtail my impulses.

Yet despite all my penance, I still could not shake the fear of acting out as a sexual predator. And for very good reason; forgiveness, as it turns out, is not an anti-dote for a shame-stained self-image. In fact, it has the contrary effect of reinforcing falsely assumed guilt. I did not need forgiveness for the fact that my innocence was stolen. I needed the assurance that it was not my fault and that I deserved to loved, not punished.

I could not find that assurance anywhere in my religious teachings.

IN SEARCH OF COMMUNITY

Most men lead lives of quiet desperation.

Henry David Thoreau

The time had come to test my mettle as a pastor, the opportunity to move from *promise* and *potential* to *actual*. I took my calling to this little prairie congregation with utmost seriousness and dedication.

Following the detailed directions given us by the pastoral selection committee, we took the faintly marked exit off the Transcanada at Grierson corner, followed the road east and then turned north at the sign pointing to Drumheller. (In this part of the world all roads lead to Drumheller.) It was a warm, sunny, dry July afternoon, the kind of weather we would learn to expect. A perfect climate, unless you were a farmer or someone living in a farming community dependent on the generosity of farmers, like we were. Here, weather was a much more critical issue than whether it would be a good weekend for a ball tournament or picnic.

The entrance to Little Denmark was about as auspicious as one would expect for a prairie town of 350 people. There was one main street, with the Co-op grocery store, a post office, the bank, a hotel with a bar and the Chinese restaurant, a curling rink, a ball diamond, a playground and a Rec centre. There was also a public school and high school. Throw in a small industrial complex which included a fertilizer plant, and that pretty much summed up the town. And of course, the Lutheran Church, white ship-lapped with steeple and black roof and stained oak doors, built when the first

Danish settlers had arrived from Michigan in the 1920s. Much of the area was still farmed by their descendants.

We pulled into the driveway of the church manse next door to the church. It was a spacious, attractive stucco bungalow with an immense lot occupying half the block. Beth took the children outside to explore. I took a quick look about inside to get my bearings, and then up the precariously steep stairs (designed after the *ladder-to-the-hay-loft* motif) to the second floor and flopped down onto the ready-made bed with as much impropriety as Goldilocks. The sun was shaded by a large poplar tree out the west window. Songbirds filled the branches. There were no traffic noises, no dogs barking, just peace and tranquillity. As I settled down into a deep sleep, all the weight and stress of travel and past disappointments and excitement and anticipation of future promise drifted out the window and was carried away across the expansiveness of the Alberta prairie. It was an hour and a half before I awoke refreshed, ready to start life anew.

We needed a fresh, new start. Not that we hadn't had our share to this point. Beth and I had travelled the country from one coast to the other, moving a dozen times in a dozen years, attempting to find a situation that suited our individual aspirations and afforded enough common ground on which to grow a marriage and family. To date, those elusive qualities of happiness and companionship had eluded us. Now we were trying again, (a last-ditch effort, if truth be known), but this time with all the special ingredients that had previously been missing. We had two delightful children and a beautiful home in a quiet country setting – the ideal environment for raising a young family. Beth would have her dream as the stay-at-home wife of a Lutheran pastor. I would have my first solo pastorate. This was our first chance for a real home.

Novice pastors are often given rural charges as testing grounds. The work load is not too demanding and the congregation is typically seasoned and stable enough to give guidance to a young pastor and keep him from screwing up. If, in fact, he or she falls by the way, the damage is contained within the smaller community. We were assured before accepting the call that this congregation was solid enough that it would straighten out whatever curves we might throw their way. A good thing. Their mettle would be tested soon enough and more exhaustively than anyone would have anticipated or desired.

The first evening, as if to calm any apprehension, Verna and Albert, an older couple that we grew to love and count on for support, made a brief stop by with a steaming apple pie to welcome us.

"It's so good to see the lights on in the parsonage again, Pastor," Albert stated in his warm, comforting voice. Apparently, to make people happy it was enough just to turn the lights on! That we could do.

Mid-morning of the following day, another knock on the door. This was not a simple greeting call. Standing on the front step, hat in hand, were the president of the congregation and a parish member from three doors down. Her father had died the day of our arrival and funeral services would be required. There were certainly the sincerest of apologies on their part for having to press me into service so quickly and for the awkwardness of my not having known the deceased. For my part, I was delighted to be needed. I sensitively and creatively wove together stories that honoured the old gentleman, though he was somewhat of a recluse and certainly no frequenter of the church.

This ability to personalize the funeral around the unique gifts and character of the deceased won sincere and lasting gratitude from the community. Death and dying pulled together all the dominant themes of Lutheranism, as well as the concerns of small-town Alberta. Funerals became the mainstay of my ministry during my tenure there. Years later, when congregational and community members would gather to comment about my failings as a pastor, someone would often add in closing, "But he does a great job at funerals."

Little Denmark initially attracted Beth and me as the coveted opportunity to belong to a community. It was small, rural, and homogeneous. Everyone at least knew each other if they weren't related. These were the most hospitable people you could hope to meet: pleasant, kind, faultlessly polite, and neat, (Did I mention neat?), virtues that they retained from the home country, distilled and intensified through the generations since settling here from Denmark. The elderly of the community were very supportive and quick to embrace a new pastor and his family, doing everything they could to make us feel at home.

Despite this valiant effort, it was not home. It was like nothing I had experienced before. It was a different way of communicating, different values, distinctive traditions. It felt like being in a foreign mission field, for which I had neither applied nor done the prerequisite cross-cultural communication training. Call it a *parachute pastorate*: being dropped in from the sky with no ground support.

The first Sunday we arrived, we were introduced to congregational life by an elderly male choir director and an all-female choir (young Danish farm girls, good stock). Here was one of the last places in the Free World where the *order of creation* was carefully preserved, with one man giving leadership and a whole choir loft of women responding obediently to his every gesture. These anachronisms would surface at the most unexpected moments and in the most peculiar fashion. Another Sunday, after a baptismal service, Beth and I were invited to the reception after the service. On entering the house, I was directed downstairs to mix with the men while the women stayed upstairs close to the kitchen. This arrangement was repeated at public gatherings, again with the men in one section and the women in the other.

We did make a sincere attempt to blend in. One attempt involved my driving a tractor around a field with a fallow rig of some sort in tow. Not one for paying attention to details, I left wide swaths untilled. I was not asked back. Ditto the time I offered to assist in fence repair but couldn't hammer in the eight-inch spike. Another failure. I started playing hockey and injured my knee when I threw an illegal check. Curling involved some questionable social dynamics and a fair bit of drinking after the games, so I bowed out.

This small rural ethnic community seemed to draw into focus and crystallize every insecurity and unresolved issue I had acquired to that point. Take marriage, for instance. In my first year in this small community, I must have blessed half a dozen 50th wedding anniversaries and one 60th! I had always believed that if I stuck my marriage out long enough, there would be a pot at the end of the rainbow: one morning I would wake up after 50 years of tension and tedium and realize that I had actually grown emotionally close to the woman sleeping next to me. Then it would all make sense and all the unhappiness and discomfort that we had been through to that point would have been worthwhile. Now I was seeing what a marriage of 50 or 60 years looked like. This wasn't fine wine or single malt whiskey; there was no guarantee that anything got any better with age.

SHOWERS OF BLESSING

Last night the rain
spoke to me
slowly, saying,
what joy to come falling
out of the brisk cloud,
to be happy again
in a new way
on the earth!

Mary Oliver, *Last Night the Rain Spoke to Me*

On just another October night, driving home from Calgary, I turned off the highway into the descending darkness of a country road, the air reddened with the thick musky scent of grain dust. I watched the sluggish, persistent march of the combines into the fading evening light until, save for the solitary headlights peering into the dusky dark, they were consumed by the blackness.

What compelled these care-takers of the land to give their heart and soul to this unrelenting, seemingly thankless lifestyle? All the year through they would drive up and down the dirt roads along their fields, marking and measuring the depth of the snow, then the moisture in the soil, then the sprouting of the crops, one eye fixed on the earth, the other to the heavens. It was not an occupation: it was an obsession.

The years that we lived in that small community were marked by the continuation of a drought that had lasted for a decade. Each spring, after heart and hope was seeded in the soil, the anxiety would slowly mount as the horizon was scanned for signs of moisture. In town the intensity of the conversations would mirror the stresses of the crop year.

"Lars got .5 inch up on the ridge last week."

"Yeah, while nothing has come my way for months."

"How much longer do you think we have before we write this year off?"

"It is certainly getting to that point. Haven't seen a sprout yet."

It was early June, 1989. It had been a dry winter and virtually no moisture at all in the spring. The despair and desperation ran as deep as the furrows in the parched fields. A dust storm kicked up for a few days and a friend had close to a half inch of topsoil on the inside of her windowsills. If not for the advancement in tilling practices, the loss of soil would have been worse than in the Dirty Thirties.

But then the wind shifted. Someone reported that a weather front was starting to build south of the border several hundred miles away. The conversation remained guarded and tentative, as if too much enthusiasm or hope would jinx the last hope of this crop year. But as it continued to creep up slowly from Montana and through the southern foothills it became impossible to quell the nervous excitement.

On the third day, the morning sky was layered with a thick dark blanket of moisture. The heavy laden clouds seemed to just be hanging there, teasing, almost defying hope. For awhile, it looked like they might move past to the west, missing the desperate community altogether. Around five a.m. on the fourth day, a light pitter-patter began resonating through the early morning dawn: no fanfare of thunder and lightening or sudden downpour, just a soft misty cover over the community.

It is said that the Inuit have fifty words for snow. Farmers need the same range of vocabulary for rain. Some rain can fall hard and wash away the dusty topsoil, doing more harm than good. Some rain falls too lightly and pools like droplets of oil on a silky base, barely penetrating. Some rain evaporates in the heat, the veil of moisture hanging suspended above the hot earth, full of promise but no substance. This rain was none of those. It soaked into the thirsty ground, gently massaging and healing the parched, cracked soil. Not a drop was wasted over the ensuing three days of rain. No water ran in the gutters or pooled alongside the road, no topsoil washed away. The earth was satiated, the crops nurtured, the heart and faith of the community restored.

But these showers of blessing were mostly anecdotal. The drought continued and the pressures on the family farm continued to mount. *Agriculture* was being displaced by *agribusiness*. Farms became larger than ever imagined – five, six, seven sections. New combines cost hundreds of thousands of dollars. Banks insisted that security for the home quarter be surrendered as collateral for the loans, leaving the family no security in the event of rising costs and falling grain prices. Banks called in the loans on any commercial operations that showed signs of floundering and sold off inventories ten cents on the dollar. Communities shrank as fewer people were needed to work the larger machinery. The families who remained were more mobile and did their shopping in larger centres, further undermining the commercial base of the community. The post office closed, then the farm equipment supply, then the gas station. The life blood was being slowly leeched out. Even the Chinese restaurant closed. (What is a prairie town without a Chinese restaurant?)

Through it all the Church stood as a testament to the tradition and roots of the community. Fear of the changing outside world intensified loyalty to the old ways and resistance to the new. Religion endured as a buttress against the creeping dissolution of traditional values and way of life.

And so, every Sunday morning, those same men and women who had been on the tractor until two in the morning the night before, were up bright and early to set the altar for communion or to hand out bulletins, or to sing in the choir, ensuring that their soul was tended to as carefully as the soil, thankful to a God who long ago promised that as a reward for their meekness they would one day inherit the earth.

This is the social function of a rural church: to preserve the timeless rituals and the connection with the Motherland. Faith is manifested in maintaining the old world order. Other pastors would have welcomed this traditional form of religious life. I didn't. My sense of ministry was to incite change, to challenge the status quo, upset the powers that be, raise a little hell. That I did. It wasn't a good fit.

Every Sunday I would put forth my best effort to bring about some change. I railed against the evils and injustices of society for 15 to 20 minutes, and then, for the next 40 minutes attempted to put them right through the prayers and liturgy. "For one brief shining moment," the grace of God would wipe the slate clean of all the evils of humanity and restore this confused, conflicted, scarred planet to the mythical purity of Eden or Camelot. Then reality would set back in, and we would all return to our lives of quiet desperation. Was it unreasonable to expect a little shift, a micro-adjustment in mentality, a small something that indicated the Gospel was having some impact?

⚜ TANGO INTERLUDE

Showtime! It had been a year and a half since our engagement and simultaneous entrapment by tango. Our embrace continued to *intensify* during that time until we sealed the deal by setting a wedding date.

The natural location was of course, LaBoheme, not only because of the tango connection but because it was sufficiently *bohemian* to host our eclectic social circle and bizarre wedding ceremony. This included a wedding march serenaded by drum beats and a didgery-doo (!) and culminated in two tango demonstrations one by Ernst and Tamara and one by Patricia and I. We had been re-hearsing for the past two months under the tutelage of Vicente and Christina. Although we broke Ernst's cardinal rule by thoroughly choreographing our dance, what it lacked in spontaneity it made up for in raw emotion.

All this passion was all eloquently encapsulated in a poem written by Patricia for the occasion:

Love at Mid-Life.

Love at mid-life
Comes dressed in the creases and folds
Of skin that has weathered
Births and deaths,
Seasons of storms,
Seasons of calm and seasons of solitude.

Mature love slips in
On the wings of Grace
When you know yourself
To be complete in your aloneness.

Love at mid-life invites you into a passionate dance
While calling a truce to the games and dramas of young love.
Seasoned love whispers in your ear
"You can do this"
"You have so much to give."
"You deserve so much to receive what is offered."

And blushing,
You hold out your trembling hand and say
"I do."

OPENING TO LOVE

By this point I was coming to the conclusion that mindlessly mumbling, *"I, a poor miserable sinner,"* was not engendering a general sense of well-being. Loving the unlovable may have been the right formula to make *God look good*, but it never made *me feel good*.

I might have suffocated under this blanket of spiritual paralysis save for the intrusion of several life-altering realizations headed my way. One was the teachings of theologians such as Matthew Fox who countered the doctrine of *original sin* with *original* blessing, the notion that we were created and remain at the core, good, pure, and loveable.

There is a basic tenet of psychology which asserts that to be able to give love, we must be able to receive it as well, à la, "Love your neighbour as you love yourself" (more red-letter print). In fact, trying to receive or retain anyone's love, God's included, without positive self-esteem is like trying to contain water in a sieve. My spirit was perforated with self-hate punctures. I was leaking love at every turn, never able to keep any of it for myself.

I was longing for the searching eyes of God to look deep into my soul, to see me as I truly was and say something other than "poor miserable sinner." Perhaps something like: "Behold my beloved son, in whom I am well pleased." Were all the *kudos* reserved for Jesus? Apparently, God's love could only be experienced in the context of self-loathing.

This negative self-image one day almost got ditched, literally. I was driving into Calgary, listening to an inspirational tape that a colleague had made. At one point my colleague instructed, "Look in the mirror and tell yourself that you are beautiful." The only mirror that I had available was the rear-view mirror. I had to adjust it to see my reflection and repeat that positive affirmation: "I am a perfect and beautiful creation of God." I almost drove off the road! What I was saying definitely wasn't matching with what I was seeing. I lived from a mental model of being incomplete, inadequate and even ugly at a soul level. My life work was to get me fixed up into something that was acceptable and presentable to God.

The prospect of letting myself off the hook and soaking up a little unconditional love terrified me. It would derail my drive for self-improvement and perfection. What if I started seeing good in the world rather than evil? Where would I look? What would I see?

The opportunity was being presented to see the essential beauty of the me that is created in God's image. My spiritual orientation was shifting from what was wrong with me and the world around me, where God isn't, to seeing where God is and recognizing the Divine Presence in everything. This invited looking within and without from eyes of love, seeking out the good and the beautiful, believing that everything has originated from and is permeated and sustained by that same Divine Spirit.

I determined to go in search for love wherever I could find it. To this point in life, I had had little to encourage or direct me in this quest. There was no guarantee that God or anyone else would lead or follow. Certainly the Church wouldn't. If I had to go it alone, so be it. Staying the course was no longer an option.

The second disruption I feared the most, namely the intrusion into my life of real, full-bodied love, love that coursed through ones veins and impassioned and enlivened, love that in the end felt much more divine that the dispassionate resolve to love the unlovable. The seeds of this awakening were sown with the arrival of our first child and then blossomed fully with our second child two years later. I had only to stand back and marvel as this miracle unfolded. Everything about them was a thrill: poking through their bowel movements, listening for the crude body noises, taking photos of their faces smeared with food. They were beautiful little creatures and I embraced this opportunity to love them as exhaustively as I could. Parenting immediately became the biggest privilege and priority of my life.

Andrew was twelve years coming and well worth the wait. Being a proud and devoted father quickly became my *raison d'être*. I never tired of carrying him or caring for him or showing him off. We arranged our entire social calendar around the sleeping and feeding times of our new addition, not worrying about inconveniencing anyone else. At night I was attentive to his every whimper, running to his side the instant he made a sound. Classic first-time parenting syndrome.

Andrew was a very mild-mannered child, who loved his order and routine. Bright and alert, he was attentive to the most intricate details. I would read to him long books and then change a word every now and then to trick him. He caught me every time. He was fascinated with anything mechanical and electrical and would horrify other parents with his passion for plugging and unplugging electrical appliances. "I plug it in. I plug it out," he would state proudly.

In the early years, Andrew's countenance often exhibited an almost translucent quality, to the point where I sometimes barely recognized him. As the years wore on, I suspect this thin veil exposed too much vulnerability and his bright, cheerful disposition was displaced by a certain melancholy and dullness. No doubt the home troubles added to this estrangement.

Amelia came two years less one day later. Same zodiac sign but couldn't have been more different. Amelia was an extreme extrovert, always seeking to be the centre of attention. Where Andrew was quiet and reserved, Amelia was boisterous and flamboyant. She loved being the pastor's daughter and the attention that came with it. If there was someone taking a picture, she would run headlong into the lens. Andrew would run and hide. She carried her heart on her sleeve and would often as not cry herself to sleep. Not colicky, she just had a lot of emotional energy to release. That never changed, nor did her desire to be in the limelight.

It was as if my heart was opened for the first time with love as a feeling, a desire to have fun, to play, to want nothing more than to be in their company and expect nothing else in return. Up to that point, my notion of love, supported by good Christian theology, equalled *putting up* with and *suffering through*. But here I was loving my children not *in spite of* but *because of*. This love wasn't sustained by will power and commitment in overlooking their flaws and limitations: I couldn't find flaws! Everything about them was a sheer delight. They were absolutely perfect! This was the most natural, powerful energy that I could imagine. It was deeply addictive and I wanted my life to be full of it. There was definitely a need to create more *soul space*.

DUST DEVILS

They sentenced me to twenty years of boredom
For trying to change the system from within.

Leonard Cohen, *First We Take Manhattan*

On a hot, summer day, I sit down on the back step of the church manse in contemplation, searching for an answer to my disillusionment, peering down the dirt lane to the rolling hills that defined the horizon on the west end of town. A small dust devil flares up and dances ecstatically down the road and then quickly vanishes. My tired mind begins to make random associations between that visual and ministry in a small prairie town: a quick flourish then vaporising with no lasting effect – other than to cause a little disruption on an otherwise serene prairie landscape. The hopes and dreams, shame and grief are whipped up like dust from a ditch and then strewn with abandon across a vacant field.

A wise Jesuit priest encouraged his parishioners to have a *global meltdown* by mid-life to dethrone the tyrant ego, so that one could then get on with the task of rebuilding one's life on more solid footing. I was apparently right on schedule. Conflict was erupting in every corner of my life: in my marriage, the church, my relationships, my faith and religious devotion, all a consequence of having ignored for so long the psyche's need for balance and expression.

Mid-life deconstruction is high-octane iconoclasm, involving not only a restructuring of life circumstance but also of faith and the psyche. Confronting the delusions that have formed the foundation of one's self-esteem and social presence requires fierce courage, reckless abandon and a desperate desire to save one's soul above all else. Nothing is safe or sacrosanct. No tenets are unquestionable, no idols nailed down. It requires letting go of all securely held beliefs about one's self and the world. It is a time of razing everything to the ground, allowing oneself the blessed opportunity to rebuild from the bottom up, the thrill of starting with a clean slate.

Embarking on this journey of self-discovery was both uninvited and unavoidable. I had invested twenty years cocooning myself in a belief system and lifestyle because of the protection and security that they promised. This intransigence in dealing sensitively with my inner world was further exacerbated by becoming a pastor. Whatever space there had been before for honest self-reflection and exploration was now completely stultified. The camel-hair cloak I had donned of the resident holy man afforded no room for being both vulnerable and venerable.

In the end, this spiritual straightjacket was not enough to insulate me, either from the toxicity of my past or the passion of the present, despite my best efforts.

THE MYSTICAL FOREST

*Every leaf of the tree becomes a page of the sacred
scripture once the soul has learned to read.*

Sa'di Shiraz, Sufi Master (1213-93).

In an attempt to restore equilibrium, I set off in search of a spiritual director, starting with the Yellow Pages and ending with Glen, a Christian pastor, a soft-spoken, gentle sort, understanding and supportive and a bit of a *free spirit* himself. I met with him once or twice a month for about a year in the hopes of gaining some stability in my life. For better or worse, that was not to be.

In the middle of one visit, when we were attempting to sort through all the confusion and turmoil that I was experiencing in my ministry and marriage, he confronted me with a simple question, "What would God have you do with your life right now?"

I expected to hear myself recite a programmed response, à la, "Sell everything and give it to the poor and go be a missionary in Africa." Instead I blurted out, "It has something to do with those trees."

"Trees? What trees?" he asked, a reasonable reaction to my peculiar pronouncement.

"I am not really sure. I guess it must be the trees out back of the parsonage." There was a grove of ash trees, about seven rows with about fifteen trees in each row, neat and orderly in good Danish fashion. Although planted about fifty years earlier, they were all still relatively healthy. The trees were not big or impressive in stature, in many cases they were little more than shrubs. No doubt that was their survival strategy through the years of drought.

"I have been conceiving a plan where I would build sort of a devotional walk up and down the rows. Put out a few benches, statues, plant some flowers. Maybe a fountain. Of course all this takes time and money."

He interjected, "I think you should be out in the trees right now."

I protested, "It's winter. The trees are bare. I don't even have a bench in place where I could sit and time my meditations." I always logged the time, in case God failed to notice.

"I don't think that is the point. I think you need to learn how to just be with the trees. Relax with them. Be present. Listen. Don't take any agenda or have any expectations."

Several internal alarms were set off. Prior to becoming a born-again Christian, I had developed a deep spirit bond with the great outdoors. It was a receptive canvas on which to project my inner landscape, devoid of troubles and full of enchantment. I would pass evenings, even weekends, camping outdoors, looking up into the stars, entranced by the expansiveness of it all.

But the connection went deeper than that. One summer afternoon, in my mid-teens, I rescued a copy of The Weekend Magazine blowing across our front lawn that had on its cover a picture of a rose in full bloom, covered in snow. The article was about Findhorn, a community in one of the most inhospitable parts of Scotland that boasted some of the most remarkable gardens in the British Isles. Those botanical miracles, such as domestic roses blooming in mid-winter on a sandy beach on the wind-blown tip of Scotland – so austere a place it is difficult to understand how even humans live there (or why) – were credited to the efforts of Nature Spirits: faeries, fauns and the like. As bizarre as this claim seems, it rekindled a knowing from childhood that all the world is full of Spirit and populated with little creatures which fill the mind with fancy and the soul with mystery.

My theological training dispelled all those silly notions. Communing with trees or nature, in whatever form, was paganism. There were no spirits in the natural world, good, bad or otherwise, not in rocks or trees or rivers or animals, and definitely no little faerie-like creatures to populate the wild. Lutherans were even stingy when it came to acknowledging angels! There is only one true Spirit, the Holy Spirit, channelled through Word and Sacrament on Sunday a.m. between the holy hours of 11:00 a.m. to 12:00 p.m. and it has nothing to do with Nature but everything to do with a temperature-controlled, properly vented sanctuary with insipid wine and pasty wafers. I preached many a sermon against delinquent members who thought they could worship God equally well on the golf course or at their favourite fishing hole during that holy hour when they should have been in church.

Despite these misgivings, I was paying my counsellor good money for his advice and so agreed to comply. I definitely got my money's worth. In short order, my most profound experiences would no longer be the made-in-church variety but part of the great natural arena of Creation, more specifically my back yard. My insular, thermostatically-controlled spirituality was about to have its doors blown open.

The first time I began to just *be* among the trees, rather than busily *doing* something about them, the grove began to present itself as sacred place, holy ground. Previously, I had been preoccupied with pruning, tilling, watering – whatever it took to get them presentable for God and me. When I began to walk among them in simple awareness, I immediately got the sense that I was there as a guest, not a gardener; an observer, not a fixer. It was not my right or responsibility to envision how they should look to suit me. They were already the way God intended. Respect was paramount. I was not to be cutting or hacking or burning. Although many of them were half dead, the upper branches dried and knurled, none of this mattered when I learned to be present in acceptance and awareness.

The experience of being among the trees quite quickly evolved into a deep communion. A communication link was being fashioned between what was going on inside and what I saw and felt around me. I began to get messages from the trees, in a type of divination process as the trees cast a shadow on the snow under the moonlight. By standing with a shadow for a time, I would gain a sense what message it might be relaying. It was like being in a waking dream. Night after night, I would walk among the trees and be amazed at the variations of the shadows, the moon creating pictures and images in the snow. The entire grove became enchanted. Every walk was a new adventure into the mystical. It would shock me that an image so vivid and obvious one night had not been apparent the night before. The dead trees often cast the most intriguing patterns – the barren branches, like long fingers on the end of long knobbly arms and elbows, encrypting the message of the evening.

I was right back into the thick of the Musical Forest with my friend Howdy Doody.

In this exercise of tree divination, the attitude of approach was everything. It became clear to me, through trial and error, that if I was to gain anything from this process, I was not to take responsibility for what I received. I had to learn to accept the messages as gift. My egotistic reasoning would forever want to jump into the middle and claim credit for all the insights, as if I were projecting my thoughts onto the trees or reading messages into the shadow patterns. The problem was, whenever I gave this very logical line of reasoning any credence, the insights would immediately stop. The trees were talking. I had to learn to shut my mind up and listen.

The first tree I confronted on my walks was the *witching tree*. It tested my attitude to ensure that I was in a suitable frame of mind for entering. It was the gatekeeper to the mystery of the sacred grove, my entrance to the adventure. Her shadows enfolded me, almost sensually caressing me, arousing my sense of mystery and lulling me into receptiveness. There were several almost ladder-like shadow steps that she cast, sometimes resembling a keyhole, other times a heart. I would be required to carefully step through these shadows, often having to pause for a lengthy period of time until I surrendered my judgement and cynicism at the door and was worthy to proceed.

Certain trees represented elements of community life. It was a nightly challenge to make it through the low branches of the cen-soring trees before getting to a friendlier tree that offered shelter and acceptance.

It was often quite an emotionally intense experience acting out this journey. The message was typically a whole-body experience, transporting me into some other consciousness. One evening, one of the shadow patterns represented a stag. I drew into myself the strong male deer energy and began to prance through the forest as this proud and dignified character. Another evening, something suggested a wolf and I raged through the wood with the fierceness of the cunning and powerful carnivore.

These psycho-dramas were not only cathartic but also brought insight and strength, affirming my choices, giving direction, in-spiring courage. On a particularly dark night, I was carrying a deep sense of regret from my wayward heart that was forever creating complications. At the end of my walk, I was startled by a tree cast-ing the most intricate, delicate lace-like patterns on the snow. The meaning was instantly obvious to me: they were veins and this was "the blood of Jesus that cleanses all sins!" It was so vivid that I was amazed I had never seen it before. Nor did I again. But for that few minutes, I bathed in the cleansing shadow, as clean and white as the snow beneath. The biblical verse played over in my mind:

"Though your sins be as scarlet, they shall be as white as snow; though they be red like crimson, they shall be as wool."

A cold winter's day had left the thinnest skiff of snow on top of the hard crust beneath. It was dead calm with only the lightest puff of wind that would manifest from nowhere and whip the powder into a little whirling devil. Then as quickly as it had arisen, the snow would settle in its new location. This happened sporadically and unpredictably throughout my walk that night. It presented the perfect image for spirituality: lying motionless, weightless, instinctively responsive, waiting for the breath of God to stir one to life.

INTO THE SHADOW

If one only learns to deal with his own shadow he has done something real for the world.

Carl Jung, *Psychology and Religion.*

Opening up to the intuitive and psychic, which was neither filtered by intellect nor censored by convention, was as profound and disruptive as I feared it might be. My rigid belief system that was desperately trying to maintain a grip on reality and preserve the rightful order of all things (read: status quo) was being shouted down by heretical inner counsel attempting to lay claim to my consciousness. Somehow, I would have to pull myself together before I totally fell apart.

Rummaging further through my *bag of alternative resources*, I extracted cassettes of John Bradshaw elucidating the dynamics of shame in family systems and the need to nurture the *wounded inner child*, Joan Borysenko, deconstructing shame and guilt, Virginia Satir teaching positive self-esteem, Robert Bly beating the drum of the *men's movement*, Reanne Eisler honouring the Goddess and sacred pleasure, medicine cards which outline Aboriginal teaching about totem animals and assorted Gaya-centred liturgies, astrology readings and other eclectic philosophies.

In addition to this reading, I uncovered a dog-eared textbook on Jungian psychoanalytic theory. It diagnosed the root of my inner conflict as dissociation from my *Shadow*, that part of the *Self* that harbours instinctual behaviours, primal life force and other disruptive and unsophisticated personality traits. Naturally, as a representative of proper society I had made every effort to repress and distance myself from this shadow realm that was presumably the domain of the devil, the hothouse for the sins of the flesh.

The outcome of this position was to be trapped in the classic *spirit versus flesh* dichotomy, with no bridge for integrating a wholesome bodily awareness with intimacy and sensuality. In its stead was supplanted an antiseptic and sterile piety. Not exactly a life-enhancing outcome, which was precisely Jung's point: the further we distance ourselves from our shadow, the more devoid we are of passion and power.

But the more serious offence, from Jung's point of view, was the non-acknowledgement of the Self, the directing force that guides one through the life process of *individuation* to growth and wisdom. It is the Self, not the ego or will or intellect (all those attributes that we assume define our true nature and direct our life's path) that over the long haul calls the shots. If one's ego-needs for self-control and self-aggrandizement are resisting the inner urge to deeper understanding and self-actualization, then the Self steps in and resets the course. If one is attuned to the promptings of Self or Spirit, then this process can be gentle and gradual. However, if one's ego digs in its heels, as in my case, then the Self has to mastermind a coup of sorts. This approach is typically not pretty, although the outcome can be life-sustaining.

Although the long-term outcome of this soul-searching promised to be mental and spiritual health, the immediate consequence was further fragmentation of my psyche. I was typically of two or three minds, all seemingly at cross-purposes playing out like a multiple personality disorder, with contradictory influences and impulses dogging my every action and thought.

In response to this cacophony of counsel, imaginary characters began to materialize as metaphors for the conflicting aspects of my psyche - *Monkey, Fox and Raven* - each jostling to represent their respective interests and perspectives.

Fox emerged into my adult consciousness during a vision quest in the hoodoos off the Red Deer River. He sporadically darted in and out of creases and crevices, modelling the conflicting qualities of courage, conviction and cowardice with which I wrestled.

As my connection to all things moral and upright, Fox is the epitome of propriety and civility. He committed himself in earnest to being the good boy, saying the right things, staying out of trouble. I sensed I could count on Foxy to watch my back and give me very useful counsel on things that mattered, namely how to preserve my comforts, authority and prestige in the community, (all of which were at this time very much in jeopardy).

Fox at this time, is curled up in the corner, tail over his face. Out of respect, I resist the impulse to pick him up and coddle him. If not entirely wild, he is certainly shy.

"And to whom do I owe the honour," say I, giving a nod of acknowledgement.

"Freddie's the name, sir," Fox responds courteously.

"Interesting," I muse. Freddie is also my name, after a friend of my father who in addition to other undesirable traits, was a child molester. How intricately and inseparably the blemishes of my childhood were interwoven with my adult world. "So you have inherited my *name of shame*," I say to Freddie, determining at that moment that I would refer to him as Foxy.

Monkey surfaced as part of my psychological makeup with the advent of adolescent hormones, but did not get a proper introduction until a Mayan astrological reading much later in life, informed me that Monkey, Artist and the Trickster were my astrological signs.

"Don't I ever get a break?" I protested. "I just want to be good!"

Having Monkey in one's *spread* definitely precludes against this outcome. Monkey is pure uncut energy, raw libido, sensuality and sexuality, wild, reckless, fun-loving and free, as well as many other equally unsophisticated attributes, all the primal instincts that, in my religious devotion, I attempted to repress. Consider, for instance, the instinctual primate behaviour for marking territory: loud offensive vocalizations or smells, depending on the situation and the intended effect.

"Come on, tell the whole story. I don't just go around belching and farting all over the place," objects Monkey.

"Right. Of course not. How thoughtless of me."

For better or worse, there are whole other dimensions to Monkey. "Let's hear it for Monkey the Party Animal, wild, reckless and fun-loving, committing thoughtless, inane acts simply for amusement," I offer disheartedly.

In fact, the more I attempted to act proper and keep Foxy centre stage, Monkey would sally out from behind, like a bad case of *Tourette's*. Consider when I was a cub-scout leader on a church youth group camp-out and intentionally dropped my underwear into the cooking pot of water. Or at a family birthday party, playing soccer in a public park, when I took a plastic cone-shaped pylon and stuck it down my pants to use as a protective cup (quite a visual!). I had to be told by one of the children – more mature than I at half the age – that this was inappropriate. Or officiating at a wedding ceremony and repeating some of the groom's private comments about the similarities between taming a woman and riding a horse. Or, in one of my sermons against the Gulf War, when I mispronounced *collateral damage* as *clitoral damage*. Monkey was so entertained with this gaffe that he repeated it throughout the week to everyone with whom I came in contact.

"And..." adds Monkey as if I were reciting a list of accolades or virtues, which in his mind, I suppose they were.

"Monkey the Sensualist," I concede with false enthusiasm.

Monkey revels in all the senses, but primarily touch. At least that is the one that caused me the most consternation. My experience had taught me that nothing caused more trouble than sex and sensuality. And nothing was more difficult to repress or redirect. I had tried to renounce the pleasures of the flesh, meditating on the lives of the Saints and Martyrs, praying to God that I would suffer from some fatal affliction that would purge me of all my wanton desires, such as contracting leprosy and having my genitalia fall off. I would have gladly accepted Monkey's lack of social graces if he would have just left sensuality out of the mix.

My adaptive strategy to preserve civility and gain respectability had been to position Foxy out front, while keeping Monkey locked up in the closet. Unfortunately, this approach inevitably led to disaster. Unacknowledged, out from under the watchful eye of my respectable self, Monkey was free to lurk around in the dark corners, venturing out at the most inopportune times, making a sham of my pretence and propriety. Poor Foxy was run ragged attempting damage control.

"Monkey, please, I have reformed," I counter. "I am tired of causing offence. From here on, I resolve to be a gentleman!" I pause and look to Foxy for support, my manifesto more a desperate plea than a confident assertion.

"Well, what are you going to do? Pretend that you don't need to have a little fun in your life?" Monkey crosses his arms, turns his back to me and farts.

I lean back against the wall, cover my face with my hands and sink to the floor in despair. There does not seem to be any acceptable compromise. I am condemned to go through life with Monkey on my back. Welcome or not, I will have to allow for the primal, instinctual and sensual in my range of self-expression.

In the background, I can hear Foxy frenetically reciting the Lutheran Confessional: "I, a poor miserable sinner, humbly confess all my sins and iniquities…"

The possible pay-off to Monkey and Fox's head-butting was that it might actually knock some sense into the situation. Enter *Raven*, just the catalyst for invoking such wisdom, Raven walks the dark path of individuation, pushing one to a deeper spirituality through the back door of pain and disruption.

With my surname *Kruk*, an Ukranian name for *Raven* (after the *krukking* vocalization it makes), I might have expected that Raven would have pitched in to help a little sooner, as wisdom was long overdue. However, Raven, always the *trickster*, takes the approach that a lesson is best learned if there is a bit of chaos and irreverence in the mix; why learn something the neat and easy way and miss an opportunity to cause embarrassment and offence along with a bit of fun?

There was one more ignoble attribute of Raven which also factored prominently in my evolution. Raven as *shape-shifter* allowed me the freedom and range to oscillate between *personas*, at one moment sanctimonious and pious, the next crude and irreverent, keeping everyone, including myself, confused and off-balance. This is not exactly a strategy for winning friends and influencing enemies, but it keeps all options open for learning and expansion.

"Kruk!" Raven sounds in his signature incantation. "At your service," head bobbing from side to side as he assesses the situation.

Knowing what I do about Raven energy, I am more than a little apprehensive about his offer. His beady eyes seem to peer deep into my malaise. I get the distinct impression that he understands more than I care for him to. No doubt he is calculating an opportunity to dismantle this constrictive environment that I have constructed. It likely won't be long in coming.

Whatever I thought of this motley crew, the task at hand was to bring all three of my alter-egos into the light, own them as an integral part of myself and hopefully socialize them somewhat in the process. As encouragement in this venture, I had only Carl Jung's teaching that I would discover in this shadow-world not the despicable and reprehensible, but a treasure chest of gold.

A BLESSED CURSE

I distinctly remember my first visit with Maggie and Don. Beth and I had been invited out to their farm about four miles out of town. It was an exceptionally beautiful evening with the sky split into crimson and cobalt, a vestige of the storm front that had just passed over. The chest deep barley and wheat waved gently in the warm wind that lingered. A brilliant double rainbow encased the drama.

As we turned into the driveway, Maggie was at the end of the driveway, greeting us with her wonderfully warm and welcoming smile. With one hand she was wildly gesturing to the rainbow, and with the other trying to keep her skirt from blowing up. My focus was alternatively flitting between the celestial artistry and Maggie's skirt flailing in the breeze. Talk about a set-up. The pattern for our relationship was more or less set at that moment. Try as I might, I would never be able to separate the physical attraction from the spiritual intrigue.

In some way, Maggie mirrored for me a long lost world for which I continually grieved. The delicate spirit of an artist was woven into her daily life, adding little touches of beauty to the world all around. She nurtured her spirit where I had been ruthless with mine. She embodied what I longed for: innocence, gentleness, and playfulness. She was able to create a world within a world, a space separated out from the commitments and worries and judgements of adult life for mixing fantasies and simple pleasures. The delight of every little experience was bewitching.

Adding to the intensity of the connection was that Maggie and I both had childhood experiences of abuse. Neither of us would have had any way of knowing this consciously at the time, but there is a strong psychic pull between people with similar childhood wounds. Another set-up.

Maggie had simple material tastes reflected in her personal appearance and dress. She had a warm infectious smile and a generous spirit. Her loves were basic: her family and her several dear friends, her connection with nature and music. "Wherever two or more were gathered" (more red-letter print), there was Leonard Cohen and Bob Dylan and Gordon Lightfoot in our midst, a folk revival of all the songs that I had banished to the subcontinent of my pre-Christian roots.

Maggie's intense sense of personal integrity often obscured an appreciation for social convention. She was often causing offence quite unintentionally, like breast-feeding her son in church. According to the community storytellers, this was supposedly designed to give me a thrill from my special viewpoint. (Is that why they have elevated pulpits?) Or like erecting a tepee in her back yard. It poked its poled top up above the flat prairie landscape, seemingly taunting those who harboured suspicions of late-night séances or pagan ceremonies. (The tepee is indeed culturally subversive, as anyone who has sat in one knows. The small entrance through which all must stoop to enter and the circle seating inside prescribe an equality and shared authority for all occupants.)

Then there was the spirit of childlikeness. Maggie loved children and played as freely, indulging herself in childish pranks and ventures just because it pleased her. On Saint Patrick's Day, she coerced me into dressing up as a leprechaun and disrupting the classes in the local school. (Fortunately, I was well enough costumed that no one recognized me.) All this became an invitation for my inner child to come out from hiding and to recover a sense of play and delight. The timing was critical. I was a new father and needed to learn how to enter the world of fun and imagination. Maggie and her best friend Rhonda and I and our children would spend hours in the playground across from the parsonage. These occasions of joy and happiness were too precious to miss out on, despite the optics.

Rhonda also became a very close companion in time. She embodied the warmth, hospitality and simple charm that one might idealize about farm life and farm women. Rhonda had a very deep connection with Mother Earth. She would talk with rapture about the blooming of her flowers or the harvesting of her peas. She also had boundless mothering instincts that wrapped her children and mine in the deepest warmth and respect. Rhonda's counsel was always, "Listen to your heart." For the first several years, I didn't have a clue what she was talking about. I was just becoming aware of allowing my heart to feel, and had no notion of how I should listen to it.

At the time, I interpreted my attraction to Rhonda and Maggie in the typical pietistic fashion – lust, licentiousness, debauchery – in other words, not a good thing.

"It depends on your perspective," chimes in Monkey.

"Unfortunately, perspective is something you sorely lack," adds Raven. "Attraction to the opposite sex is not always about sex, despite your childhood scripts. You have some deep emotional and psychological connections with these women. They represent so much of your life that you sacrificed to your rigid, restricted world of religion. When was the last time you sang something other than religious songs, read something other than religious books, felt something other than sanctimonious? These women represent the wild, free, open world of Spirit, something you abandoned ages ago."

"Okay, I think I can live with that," thinks Monkey, not at all sure what he understood, other than the "wild, open, free" part.

"Well, I can't," objects Foxy, chilling at the suggestion. "That is why we have faith in the first place, to protect us from getting swept up in all that sentimentality and sensuality. It will undo everything we worked for, in short order."

I could certainly agree with Raven that I lacked perspective. It felt like flying off into a deep fog on autopilot. I had no idea where I was headed or if a safe landing was remotely possible.

PSYCHIC SUPPORT

Having responded to his own call, and continuing to follow courageously as the consequences unfold, the hero finds all the forces of the unconscious at his side.... One has only to know and trust, and the ageless guardians will appear.

Joseph Campbell, *The Hero with a Thousand Faces.*

In the meantime, support for this madcap adventure came from the most unexpected places. There was Helen, the psychic, who had just been evicted from a sister Lutheran Church and came to me for support. She had a fascinating gift of channelling spiritual direction and gave us comforting and insightful counsel at critical times.

Then there were birds and beasts, which also got into the act. On one trip that Maggie and I were making into Calgary, we encountered a convention of hawks. There was a hawk stationed on each fence post as far as we could see, at least 150, and who knows how many on the other side of the hill! When I returned home, I reviewed the Hawk from the *Medicine Cards* (Sams and Carson):

> Right now a clue about the magic of life is being brought to you. This magic can imbue you with the power to overcome stressful or difficult situations… Hawk may be bringing you the message that you should circle over your life and examine it from a higher perspective. From this vantage point you may be able to discern the hazards which bar you from freedom of flight.

Then there was the visitation by the wolf pair. What were wolves doing in this part of the country? It was so unnatural we were shocked every time we saw them, needing to assure ourselves they weren't coyotes. They hung around for about a week in a coulee outside of Maggie's farm, showing up at opportune moments.

In Native American traditions wolves are teachers, but they

also exemplify a strong sense of community and caring for each other. Each sighting brought encouragement and seemed to come at a time when we most needed it. Then one day, they disappeared as quickly as they had arrived.

Even the appearance of something as seemingly inconsequential as a rabbit could have significance. One night, when I was supposed to stop off at Maggie's and Don's, I was considering taking the cowardly route and backing out. It would have saved having to fight my way out of the house and back in and then deal with guilt and gossip the following day. I went for a quick walk in the trees out back for some inspiration and a rabbit ran across my path.

I went back in to read the *Rabbit Card*, which was about a once mighty warrior who used to take counsel with the tribal medicine woman and gain blessing from her. However, at one point he lost his courage to do so because he was afraid of her witching powers. As a consequence, she condemned him to a live his entire life in his self-limiting fear.

The card goes on to say that Rabbit's cowardice calls to himself that which he fears:

> What you resist will persist. What you fear most you will become.
> Our fears call to us the difficult lessons that we understandably try
> to avoid. The message in encountering rabbit in our path is to stop
> anticipating and worrying about the future. Accept life as under
> the guidance and protection of Great Spirit. Medicine Cards

I took that to be encouragement to not wimp out and so made the trip, apologizing for arriving late. Maggie, knowing nothing about the Rabbit Card or the reading, announced, "You were afraid to come because you think I am bewitching you and you are running from my influence. Your lack of courage will cost you spiritually."

I dream I am lying on a hearth in front of the fireplace, but a little chilled. Maggie comes by to drape a blanket over me to warm me up, very kind and thoughtful. Then she lies down behind me and snuggles in, warming and comforting. Before I know it (you know how these things go), we are lying naked together in her bed, albeit simply warming and comforting each other.

Don walks in at this time, catching us snuggling and calls me to task, "Wait until the church council hears about this," waving a slipper in the air in my direction.

I ashamedly hang my head and mutter sheepishly, "Well, my contract extension is up next week anyway," aware that this was a shallow dismissal of the deep humiliation that would result from the social censorship.

I wake from the dream, disgusted with my apologetic response to this lame, slipper-waving censorship. My relationship with Maggie was not something to demonize. Sex might have been very healing in that context, though we never found out. We retained the conviction that there were some lines that should not be crossed. Did it matter much? Maybe not, except that I knew I would not be able to maintain the facade of being monogamous if we ended in bed. There was a limit as to how far I could massage the truth.

Maggie, of course had her reasons for keeping some separation as well. She skirted around the edges of community acceptance at the best of times and this was merely ostracizing her more. Then there were also the dynamics at her home, which were no less problematic than mine.

The easiest course would have been for both of us to call it quits. It was not like this relationship had any future or was providing much current satisfaction – certainly not nearly enough to compensate for all of the aggravation it was causing. I had sidestepped many potentially amorous relationships in my married life up to that point, and could certainly have pulled out of this one. Beyond our ability to explain at the time, there seemed to be a connection which we were committed to seeing through. The dissatisfaction that each of us had with our current living situations was a contributor. Then there was the learning, growth and change that each of us was going through, for which there was no place in the community or in our marriages. But there was something more than that, less definable – inner referents that propelled us to venture together into the unknown.

No doubt I was looking for another *prima ballerina*. However, for this dance I seemed to be intentionally stepping down from the pedestal.

⅃ TANGO INTERLUDE

"Follow the line of dance!" Vince rails at me repeatedly in a futile attempt to correct my reckless tendency to zigzag across the dance floor.

"I've never followed a straight line in my life and I am not about to start now," I protest silently. Indifferent to pain and embarrassment, I have ricocheted my way through life, crashing into people and power structures along the way. Defying my teacher's instructions, I envision the line of dance twisting round and round, faster and faster in a series of ever more intricate and intertwined circles. With each twirl and swirl the dance becomes more beautiful and fluid, liberating and invigorating.

These imagings play out very well in my head but not so on the dance floor. My juvenile attempts at rewriting the rules of dance result, as predicted, in little more than a few bruised shins and egos. My dancing is far more beautiful imagined.

In reality, physicality and bodily awareness are not skills for which I had an affinity. Rooted in my childhood and reinforced with my religious training, I equated any contact with another's body with sexual advance. Dancing was listed as one of the cardinal sins, ranked right behind sex and rock music for good reason. Feelings, sensuality, physical expression were the sorts of things that got you into serious trouble. If even for a moment, you let that back beat reverberate through your body, you would lose all moral constraint along with your soul. If tango had been known in my church-going years, no doubt it would have been singled out as an example of how dance could be so hazardous to one's piety. The exquisite synthesizing of pleasure and passion, two bodies entwined, swaying rhythmically together, is everything my Sunday School teachers warned me about.

I need not to have been so frightened. Despite the presumed risks of sinking into a cesspool of licentiousness and debauchery (King James Bible cuss words), over time the effect has in fact, been quite the opposite. Oh certainly, I have skirted around the edges of fantasy and titillation, but the lasting pattern that has emerged has been to move beyond those adolescent defaults into an appreciation of the subtleties and complexities of sensuality and sexuality. I come away with a healthy respect for, rather than fear of, my body and that of my partner's. The structured confines of the dance floor provide a three-minute practicum in which I learn how to hold my body and a woman's body with respect, dignity and grace. Tango is the fiery furnace in which I confront my fears and inhibitions, knowing that I can safely walk away and leave it all behind on the dance floor.

THE MAGNIFICENT SELF

Self-doubt and self-criticism are truly arrogant – who are you to judge in any way the wonderful creature that you are? If you could see the big picture you would fall on your knees in admiration of your being and have only compassion for your humanness and struggle. Please be ever so gentle with yourself.

Gwen, *Letters*

I may not be totally perfect, but parts of me are excellent.

Ashleigh Brilliant

For reasons known only to Dr. Gwendolyn Jansma, and perhaps not even to her, she accepted an invitation from Maggie to hold an Awakening to Higher Energies workshop in Little Denmark, not exactly a hotbed of New Age thinking nor tops on the list of tour stops for spiritualist speakers. If she had made the rational decision to stay put in San Diego and tend to her psychotherapy practice, she would have spared our little hamlet a lot of disruption, and we would have been much the poorer for it.

I would never have gone except that I was dragged kicking and screaming by Maggie. I knew better. As a pastor, it was my responsibility to protest against such individualized spirituality as the breeding ground for heresy and sacrilege; instead, I was participating. I had an intuitive sense of how this would set my life on its ear.

Maggie had booked Gwen into the deluxe suite in the Little Denmark Hotel, one of six rooms atop the pool hall and bar. Down the hall there was a shared bathroom with the Chinese restaurant below (if you didn't want to eat in the bar). She must have felt like a missionary to a third-world country. As if to add insult to injury, our reservation for the workshop at the hotel down the road had been pre-empted to make space for a wedding. We were left to cram into a sitting room off the main lobby, listening to the organist play "Here Comes the Bride" next door. Definitely setting the atmosphere!

Positioned in the middle of this little sitting room was the altar. Certainly this was nothing like the altar I had come to know and treasure in our little church, encased by a communion rail padded with maroon-coloured velvet, and topped off with white brocade doilies, a candelabra, offering plates and an immense Book of Worship opened in the centre. Gwen's altar, in contrast, was a little table placed in the middle of the gathering, open and accessible to all, thoughtfully decorated with feminine touches: a silk tablecloth, a bouquet of flowers which served as the focus for meditation, candle and Gwen's prayer basket in which she gathered pictures of workshop participants. Everyone was invited to add something that was meaningful or sacred. Someone brought family pictures, someone else a piece of artwork, a crystal, a memento. It was also host to Gwen's healing amulet, which could be worn if desired, her *Blood of Christ* stone that was a dark green with red streaks through it and bags of Nordic seashell runes, which Gwen carefully and lovingly collected from the beach outside her house, dyed and painted as gifts to workshop participants.

I brought disgust and contempt. "An altar? In the middle of a hotel room? This is a sacrilege!" I protested. Altars were to be in the church with the proper rituals and adornments, sanctioned by thousands of years of religious tradition. Wars were fought over the precise formulation of these ceremonies: the chanting, the presentation of the Eucharistic elements, the reading of the scriptures. To stray from the prescribed formulas is to leave oneself open to spiritual peril (demon possession and the like). Besides, this was my territory. I had taken umpteen years of university to get sanctioned to conduct such rituals.

"Celestial traffic cop to the rescue!" mocks Raven.

Gwen's offences continued, including those typical New Age themes that I found particularly irritating: trusting one's inner wisdom, opening to intuition, *sensing the energy*. There were teachings about astrology and reincarnation and other drivel. Worse yet, she insisted on everyone assuming a posture of non-judgement and acceptance of whomever or whatever happened along one's spiritual path, since everything was under God's surveillance and direction.

"Surrender judgement? What is the congregation paying you for if not to pass judgement?" Foxy objects, the hackles standing up on the back of his neck.

"You are right, Foxy. My faith, my morality, my pastoral calling are all predicated on judgement. I am ordained to pass sentence, ferret out right from wrong, discern truth from heresy."

Raven begins to fan his wings restlessly, a sign that something is stirring within at a deeper dimension. While my theological mind and ego are reeling, my soul is entranced. I had never seen such respect and reverence shown for individual insights and experiences and personal values – and such irreverence for institutional ones! Did Gwen mean to suggest that something from my personal life, my world of feelings, experience or intuition, could be honoured and considered holy, simply because it was an expression of me? Was she going even further to suggest that there was an inner source of wisdom, an innate connection with the divine in each one of us, that could be counted on to provide one with the necessary wisdom and guidance on the spiritual path?

My heart is drawn back to the roots of my faith. It strikes me that this is, in some respects, the full playing out of the *priesthood of all believers*, the battle cry of the Reformation. A radical notion then and now, it means that all of humanity can access God directly without mediation, without someone standing in between denying or approving access. Jesus built the bridge, threw open the doors and established an indissoluble connection between the human and the divine. There are no more hoops to jump through, no rituals to master and no human gatekeepers to pay off. Just come on in.

"All the theological sophistication of The Friendly Giant," mocks Foxy. "Look up, look waaaay up."

"Watch it, Foxy. Friendly Giant is still my hero." I could use the help of the Friendly Giant right now. My spirit was being crushed under the oppressive burden of being a pastor. I had not only my confusion to deal with; the eternal destiny of the community was on my shoulders. As if to remind me of the solemnity and gravity of the situation, every morning, when I entered the sacristy, there in the middle of the altar, as bold as blood, was Jesus hanging on the cross. *Buenos dias* to you too.

Gwen, in contrast, had the amazing gift of being able to weave levity into the most intense group settings. There was nothing too sacred or sensitive that didn't invite a good dose of humour. And it was healing! There would be someone pouring out their soul in tears and she would work in a comment about snot running down their face or some such equally desensitizing and irreverent observation. The entire group, and especially the participant on centre stage, would crack up! This wasn't making light of or belittling, but inviting light into the dark places. In some peculiar fashion, it added special dignity to the process. It was as if angels and spirits flew in on the wings of the laughter and stole away the pain. Laughter, like tears, was an opening for that creative, regenerative, restorative energy that permeates life at all levels.

A central tenet of Gwen's teaching is that our true nature goes far beyond what we act out in our daily lives. When I identify with any of my social functions in life, such as father, pastor, husband, I am retreating from my deeper and more expansive identity. She challenges the participants to act out of their spiritual essence, inviting us to identify that magnificent self within.

I remember one experience in particular, sitting in the middle of the group, cuddled in Gwen's lap like a baby. She instructed me to look at the other participants as an exercise in *being seen*. My shame was so intense at the time that it was virtually impossible for me to do so. I struggled desperately through this exposure, crying violently for the next hour.

This reverence for the *holy within* extended to all aspects of the workshop. In addition to the teaching and meditation, a mainstay of the workshops was the sharing of individual stories of blessedness and woundedness. Gwen would intuit what might be the spiritual learning or the karmic energy caught up in this pain and would invite others from the group to assist with healing.

The trump card in Gwen's hand was always love and acceptance. Joseph, the holder of macho male energy for the group, once made the public confession that love was the draw that kept him coming back. He needed it and he couldn't find it anywhere else quite the same. Years later, when I had stopped attending the workshops, feeling that I had outgrown my wounded, groupie phase, it was the love that pulled me right back in.

"Strong medicine, that love," Monkey says and flits off to find a soft lap somewhere to curl up in. He quickly gets into some serious sensitivity on the other side of the room. It looks tempting.

The workshop ends with a group love-in, again standing in a circle, hand-in-hand, singing . We all hold hands and gaze around the room, making eye contact with all the other magnificent selves. Right out of the cartoons! But real. All teary eyed, we stagger around the room squeezing in as many hugs as we can before the doors close. Monkey is the last one to leave.

The internal squabbling intensifies on the ride home, Foxy and Raven shouting in either ear, one attempting to reinforce the structure that I had created and the other desperately trying to pull it down. How can I maintain my ministry and at the same time honour my inner Self, this Christ consciousness of which Gwen is speaking? For more than two years I have been attempting to straddle this ever-widening chasm between my inner world and my outer responsibilities. It was splitting me up the middle, a rather awkward and painful position.

The real problem with this whole process was that I was beginning to experience all of the social and spiritual dynamics promised by the church, outside of the church. There was nurturing here at a deep level that I was not getting from my Christian spirituality or community. The love and forgiveness are almost palpable. Gwen wisely and caringly interpreted my opposition to her openness as an expression of how desperately, at an unconscious level, I needed and yearned to be loved, seeing behind this defensive facade a frightened, wounded child.

SETTING COURSE

Within my earthly temple there's a crowd.
There's one of us that's humble; one that's proud.
There's one that's broken-hearted for his sins,
And one who, unrepentant, sits and grins.
There's one who loves his neighbour as himself,
And one who cares for naught but fame and pelf.
From much corroding care would I be free
If once I could determine which is Me.

Edward Sandford Martin, *Mixed*

"Who is the captain of this ship of fools?" I throw up my hands in exasperation. "It's time someone showed some leadership and took command of this vessel! I need some direction!"

"With all due respect, Sir, isn't that what religion is for?" Foxy offers with a touch of sarcasm.

"It is all that religion nonsense that got us into this trouble in the first place," chimes in Raven. "This journey is not about staying within the marked channels. It's about adventuring out beyond charted waters onto the high sea!" he continues.

"I love it! Adventure! A vast and belay! Baton down the hatches! Keel-haul the yardarms!" shouts Monkey.

Raven continues to expound, undistracted, "This is the hero's journey. It is about responding to our calling, fulfilling our karmic destiny. It requires courage and commitment and conviction. There is no one to prescribe rules because there are no rules."

"Hold it right there. Don't I have a say in this? I thought I was the captain." I jump in, trying to regain control of this confabulation.

Foxy looks hopeful at my assertion of authority and promptly stands to attention. "Aye, Aye, Captain! Give us our orders!"

"Yes, so what are we going to do?" questions Raven, not nearly as assured or impressed with my new-found show of conviction.

What are we going to do? Part of me desperately wants to restore order to my life and preserve the status quo, to stay with the known, the certain, to calm the waters. But I had been down that channel before. I had tried to keep the faith, tried to be good. This is where it had beached me.

"Are you sure there is nowhere that we can turn for some direction?" I look plaintively at Raven.

"Direction?" He cocks his head back and looked at me with disdain: "We make things up as we go along. This is situational ethics at its finest," he clucks. "Following someone else's direction isn't the solution. It's the problem!"

"This trusting in yourself business leads to anarchy," Foxy responds properly.

"And a little anarchy is a bad thing?" questions Raven.

I scramble feebly to Foxy's defence: "So what is going to maintain social order? What will replace religion as the opiate of the masses?" That is the first time that I had quoted Marx in defence of religion. I was obviously getting hysterical.

"This is not about the masses. This is about you," Raven continues. "The world, and your congregation, and your family too for that matter – will get along quite well without Herr Pastor. In fact, they will be much better for it in the long run. It is time to dump your social responsibilities and take the time and space you need to create some healing and wholeness."

That did indeed seem to be the essence of this journey: reclaiming personal authority and wrestling responsibility for my life and my soul out from under religious constrictions and autocracy, the same rules and regulations that I had enlisted in the past to keep me in check. Now they needed to be tossed overboard. Sure, there would be hell to pay. No doubt all the pitfalls and disasters that I had been warned about by my Sunday School teachers would befall me. But it was a journey I would have to take.

I stare around in disbelief, wondering who to credit with this new wave of reckless scheming. None of my three companions seem interested in taking responsibility. They all stare intently back at me, quite prepared at this point to follow my leadership. I seem to be setting a course even though I had no idea where I was headed, prepared to leave behind status and security and sail off in search of whatever might nourish the soul. What the hell is a *soul* anyway and why should I care this much about it? Is it more important than having a respectable job with a regular pay cheque and a stable family life?

"What does it profit if you gain the whole world but lose your soul?" quotes Raven. More red-letter print. The familiar passage gives me new-found courage.

"All hands on deck," my voice fairly booms. "We set sail immediately! Raven, to the masthead to watch for hazards." His keen eye and sense of adventure would serve well in this capacity.

"Monkey, trim the sails." This is one task that his agility and Attention Deficit Disorder were ideally suited for.

"First Mate, mark the compass," I nod to Foxy, delegating him with this rank. He is not at all impressed with my resolve to action, but he can at least be trusted to follow orders with due diligence.

"What coordinates, Captain?" he responds dutifully.

"Ah, of course. We need a course." I stammer, feeling suddenly incompetent in my newly assumed role, then quickly recover my composure. "Hard to starboard!" I bellow in a deep, authoritative, Gregory-Peck-playing-Captain-Ahab-type voice.

"There is a hazard off the starboard bow! Looks like the Bishop." Raven shouts from the crow's nest.

"Hard to port," I counter meekly.

THE ICEMAN COMETH

There are no truths, there are only stories.

Thomas King, aboriginal author

The office telephone rang. The Bishop. He needed to speak to me about some urgent church business (definitely his need, not mine). He would be at the church at 11 a.m. to discuss these matters further.

I knew to what he was referring, but it shocked me nonetheless. There had been recent sightings of impropriety, holding hands, a kiss, late-night visits at the homestead, a wistful look across a crowded room.

Under ordinary circumstances, the Bishop was a gracious and long-suffering man. He was tall, gaunt, always dressed in black clerical garb with a large cross around his neck, the external expression of his inner piety. He took his public responsibility of shepherding his flock – us pastors – very seriously. One might be cut a little slack in other jurisdictions but not under his careful watch. I liked this. From the beginning, I looked up to him as a father figure and welcomed his strength of conviction and paternalistic manner. It was precisely this type of devotional intensity that I wanted to bring to my calling. I remember his sermon at our graduation about how no pastor in his diocese would wile away their evenings watching TV nor attempt to maintain separation between public and private life. We were to be totally devout and committed to our calling every waking moment of every day.

These were somewhat different circumstances, far removed from that time of innocence. In matters of church discipline and dealing with clergy misdemeanours, the Bishop was a *take-no-prisoners* type of guy. There were already two lawsuits underway involving dismissal procedures of former clergy, and others to come. Then there were the small fry like me, who would hardly register as a blip on the radar, but a blip nonetheless that would have to be dealt with decisively.

"What did you expect? The chickens would have to come home to roost sometime. A little discretion over the past year would have helped," says Foxy, in characteristic mock sympathy.

"Better sooner than later," counters Raven, ruffling his feathers as if getting ready to preen himself. "Let's get everything out in the open and get the issues addressed once and for all." He seems to welcome the prospect of a confrontation and wanted to be looking his best for the occasion.

I almost agree with Raven. This secrecy is eating my guts out. There is a part of me that just wanted to get it over with and deal with the fallout.

Monkey begins gesticulating toward the church door. I look at my watch: 11 a.m. precisely.

The Bishop did not arrive in a good mood. He had just come away from a meeting in Calgary where he was having to deal with a very messy case of sexual abuse charges brought against a well-known and well-respected city pastor.

Cordialities were exchanged briefly at the front door. I invited Ken in to the prayer room in the narthex of the church. There was this special little space that I had set up for reflection and prayer. Inspirational posters hung on the walls, a small table with laced cloth stood in the centre with a candelabra and open Bible. A Catholic kneeler occupied one of the corners and two ornate chairs the others.

The Bishop sat in the French provincial chair next to the door.

I took my seat across from him. The small table with the white doily and the prominently displayed calligraphied Bible separated us.

The Bishop drew first: "So what is this about you having an affair." So much for civilities.

"Affair? No idea," I stammered, attempting to act surprised. To my compatriots: "Back me up on this one guys. There's nothing really I need to confess, is there?"

"What about the romp in the park?" responds Foxy.

"What about it?" I mutter defensively. "A little roll in the hay. High school stuff."

"Yeah, but you are not in high school. You are a married man and a pastor to boot," counters Foxy. "You are supposed to be done with that adolescent nonsense."

"Piss off, Foxy," snaps Monkey. "Just when we were beginning to have some fun. You screwed it up the first time round when he was a teenager with all your born-again crap."

Foxy is right – sort of. Sure, nothing really had happened, but something did happen. I remember distinctly the awareness of colours getting brighter, the air getting fresher. Life had somehow taken on a new charge, a new intensity, a new vibrancy. Call me *twitterpated*.

No doubt the Bishop would have been interested in this inner conversation, but I wasn't that eager to let him in on it. Ready to take incisive action, he would spring the trap door immediately, if required.

I quickly gather my focus and turn to the Bishop before Foxy could mount a counter-attack.

"I think people are upset about my spending too much time with fringe groups in the community," I offer. "There is a little group that meets monthly around the full moon and draws runes. No big deal really."

"If it was no big deal, why do you do it? It upsets people!" barks Foxy.

"I'll tell you why, Foxy," Raven jumps in, coming to my defence. "If we have to avoid everything that is just a little different because it doesn't fit in with the prejudices of small town Alberta, let's just shoot ourselves in the head right now rather than suffer a slow death of cranial atrophy."

"I love those full moon gatherings, sitting with Maggie under the stars," interjects Monkey, with a melancholy look in his eye.

"What about this tepee?" the Bishop pushes relentlessly.

OK. Well, he had me there. That was a little hard to dismiss. Maggie's tepee was sticking out on the bald prairie like a pimple or an erection. "It's Maggie's," I admit.

"Why does she own a tepee? Is she native?"

"No, she just likes tepees, I guess. She got a really good deal on this one." I attempt to project the image of someone rummaging through the town market on a Saturday afternoon, pricing out the different offerings of tepees, tucked in amongst the wigwams and papooses and travois.

For a moment, both of us stare at each other blankly, a little stupefied. My inane comment seemingly has a sedative effect.

"I don't have any more questions," he responds. I think the weirdness was getting a little too much for both of us. Barring the admission of any new incriminating evidence, the Bishop was quite ready to call it a day and to move on. He got up, shook my hand and then showed himself to the door.

He drove off as unceremoniously as he had arrived, leaving me to assess the damages. I pinched myself and looked around to check out the coordinates. I was still in the prayer room. Apparently, I still had a job: there had been no talk about being fired. But the secret was out. The gig was up. Whatever you wanted to call what was happening, it was no longer my private little game. Everyone had an opinion, a stake in it.

"It's your own fault," sneers Foxy. "He is being very reasonable. All he is asking for is a little public decorum. Play by the rules."

"We've done enough playing. Time to get out," concludes Raven. "Even if we have to get thrown out."

I couldn't bear to consider any outcome. My marriage, which now included two very precious little additions, and my ministry were my everything to this point in my life. This was the realization of a life dream. But it was definitely a dream that had gone sour. I was setting in motion, intentionally or otherwise, the processes necessary to extricate myself from this untenable situation.

A few months later, the Bishop made an unscheduled pastoral call to address another concern expressed by some parishioners, that of demon-possession. As one congregational member had sensitively sympathized, "The devil gets the better of all of us, at one time or another."

To anyone on the outside, it might seem ridiculous that the modern church would still take seriously the concept of demon possession. But not to the congregation or the Bishop – or me, for that matter. As a *dyed-in-the-wool* fundamentalist, I was quite willing to find something or someone else other than myself to blame for my shortcomings, à la, "The devil made me do it!" It would at least give me an excuse. What other explanation was there for my diligently cultivated piety going to hell in a hand basket? Rather than plodding deliberately along the straight and narrow path of self-control I had been accustomed to walk, I was being swept away by a lust for love and life. I suppose I could blame Raven or Monkey. No doubt reading runes under the moonlight didn't help, either.

At the time, I was quite prepared to see the intrusion of dreams, emotions, and passion into my consciousness as of the devil. Certainly, letting go of control felt to me like being in demonic territory. There is a passage in scripture I memorized all too well in my youth about a man who cleaned out his mental attic and evicted the evil spirit who had been lodging there. Unfortunately, he neglected to fill it with proper tenants, and so seven evil spirits, seeing the space vacant, claimed occupancy. In the end, the man's condition was worse than at first. I had no idea what Jesus meant by this parable (still don't) but I assumed, quite in keeping with Western rationalistic spirituality, that it was a caution against letting go of control of one's emotions, passions and thought processes. In other words, nothing could be more hazardous to one's spiritual health than to allow intuitive input from the subconscious.

Taking Jesus' instruction with utmost seriousness (Who wants to be invaded by demons: ratty hair, frothing at the mouth, unclipped toenails? Not pretty.), I committed myself to corral every idle thought and displace it with prayers or hymns or Bible verses. At one point, I calculated I had nearly a quarter of the New Testament memorized.

The Bishop did what he did best - confronting the issue dead-on with a good dose of biblical literacy. "Would you have any objection to my leading an exorcism prayer?"

My only experience with exorcisms, albeit indirect, was the movie *Rosemary's Baby*. Since I wasn't pregnant, I didn't really see what the harm would be in having our own little ritualistic exorcism.

The Bishop laid his hands on me and made the appropriate pronouncements. Foxy is skulking under the prayer kneeling bench, fearing fireworks. Raven is posted on the door, looking completely underwhelmed. Monkey climbs on top of the corner table, anticipating foul odours and convulsions.

Nothing.

"I guess that clears me of that charge," I concluded silently. Too bad. Now I have to figure out what is really going on.

"Wait a minute! I smell sulphur," says Monkey.

"Quit farting!" Raven snaps.

⚜ TANGO INTERLUDE

A stinging reprimand resurfaces from a lesson years earlier by Vicente. "You don't know how to hold a woman!"

OK. So how am I doing now? Am I presenting a firm frame, left hand extended, right arm wrapped around the mid of the woman's back, giving support and drawing her deep into my energetic space? Am I embodying self-respect, dignity and grace? Have I gained a sense of presence, reclaimed ownership over my body? Can I trust my instincts and intentions without fear that the dance will degenerate into a clutch-and-grab affair?

Reg, another instructor, identifies the principal function of the man in tango as remaining grounded, maintaining balance so that you can be there when the woman needs you to lean on. The man is the surety, the pillar. "Stop trying to read the other person's mind or be responsible for their feelings. A woman appreciates assertiveness in her man – a good old-fashioned, take-charge type of man."

Right out of a 1950's *Good Housekeeping Magazine* article on relationship etiquette. No room for this shared decision-making crap that I default to. The role of the leader and the follower are clearly defined. The styles of dance for the man and woman are in many respects polar opposites, the man showing a strong, definitive lead, masterminding the intricacies of the steps, the woman responding instantly and instinctively. The man must always know what direction the dance is to take; the woman, the reverse. Although she may know the steps and sequences well, she must dance it as if for the first time. She must *never* anticipate! Anticipating destroys the dramatic tension maintained by the split-second delay between the

lead and the follow and renders the dance perfunctory. It displaces
the freshness, creativity and element of surprise.

Let the games begin. *La Grande Seduction* is now enacted
on a dance floor with all the sensuality, subtleties and nuances.
Throughout the dance, the man is attempting to win over his partner, cultivating an atmosphere of trust and attraction. The woman
maintains her composure, for the most part, as the reluctant lover,
following with the slightest hesitation to every lead. Playing over in
the back of her mind are tapes from her upbringing which caution
her, among other things, to always keep her knees together.

The man, assuming the time-tested role of attempting to un-
dermine the woman's virtue, attempts to manoeuvre his leg between those of his partner and orchestrate a *boleo* or *gancho* or *sa-
cada*. With a little luck he springs the woman's leg free, flinging it
backward loosely, as if a rag doll. A flurried exchange follows with
each stepping over and around the other, legs entangled, until the
man's presumption is properly addressed and the woman regains
her composure and dignity.

No wonder my Baptist Sunday School teacher warned me
against the evils of dancing. Or, as Patricia said from her Catholic
perspective, "I am having to unlearn everything the nuns taught
me."

SENTENCING

My patron saint is fighting with a ghost
He's always off somewhere when I need him most.

Bob Dylan, *Abandoned Love*

It was possibly six months before the Bishop requested a personal audience again. By that time, affairs had taken a definite turn for the worse. The kisses had graduated to a definitely more *hands-on* approach. I could no longer deflect the romp in the park as a *one off*. And then there were Gwen's New Age workshops. I followed her like a puppy dog (pit bull), far outside the prescribed boundaries of church and marriage and our little town, my heart yearning for anything that resembled happiness and nurturing. From all indications, I seemed to be *pitching my tepee* outside of the ministry and my marriage, and I would have to accept the consequences.

"So let's be honest about the situation, then." Raven says, able to manipulate honesty in the most cutting fashion. "If you are not going to leave Maggie and Gwen, then leave the church and your marriage."

"Or how about just being discreet? Take Greg as an example," says Foxy, referring to a fellow pastor who had successfully navigated his way through several affairs without attracting any attention. Greg remained unscathed partly because he was in the city and partly because he had an instinct for self-preservation, something I apparently lacked. When I confided my situation to him, he was quite sympathetic for my having got into all this trouble without ever having gotten laid. "Too bad," he commiserated. "If you are getting blamed for something, you might as well have the satisfaction of being guilty."

"My point precisely," adds Monkey.

"But what is it I am hiding from?" I throw back at my comrades. "Didn't Jesus have to endure a little persecution because of the company he kept?"

"So now you're Jesus! Please," gags Foxy. "Here's an idea," he continues sarcastically: "Claim *executive privilege*. Play *one-up-manship* with the Bishop. 'You can't criticize me: I'm your boss.'"

"Heh. Two women, persecution, the whole Mary-and-Martha routine. It feels good and looks bad. What could be more like Jesus?" adds Monkey.

All the while I have one ear tuned to the front door. "Fellows, this isn't helping. The Bishop is due any minute. We have to agree on some course of action," I plead.

Too late. The crisp crunching of gravel could be heard from the church driveway, followed by a heavy, ominous thud of the church door.

I walk to the entrance with a *hung-dog* look and sullenly greet the Bishop as if he is the grim reaper. Pretty close. This time, he had come to settle the matter once and for all. We sit down in our customary positions in the newly designated execution room.

In the Bishop's hand is a formal writ compiled by the congregation, identifying all the allegations against my disintegrating ministry and marriage. He begins reading the charges in succession. "It is suggested that you are mentally and emotionally unstable."

Well, I suppose that is a step up from being demon-possessed. To say I was a little stressed was an understatement: *basket case* would be more like it. This was the most confusing and upsetting period of my life; I was unravelling at the seams and with an audience. Joy. I remember reciting *Mary had a little lamb* in one of my pastoral prayers and getting so choked up I couldn't remember how to end it. Did it or did it not follow her to school that one fateful day? Didn't Mary know that was against the rules? Such heart-wrenching drama.

Internal contradictions and doubt were permeating every level of my ministry. *Telling the old, old stories* was becoming more about my stories and less and less about Jesus. Sure, my sermons remained cloaked in Biblical drama and theological language, but woven throughout was an attempt to vilify or exorcise publicly what was haunting me privately. The more something troubled me Monday to Saturday, the harder I preached against it on Sunday.

My inappropriate personalizing of the Gospel was accentuated one Sunday when one of our fellow pastors was being sued for sexual misconduct in the parish. As pastors, we had been given an official communiqué from the Bishop to include reference to this in our sermon, making it clear that the church did not condone this sort of activity (the sexual abuse, that is, although I suspect it wasn't too fond of the suing either.) However, in my sermon I solicited understanding for this pastor, appealing to the Gospel and excusing him on the grounds that all of us are forgiven sinners and have been at some time or another guilty of similar offences.

After the sermon, one of the parishioners confronted me about my whitewashing the issue: "Call a spade a spade! This fellow was a dirty old man and he deserves to answer for his behaviour." A novel concept. My childhood reflex of excusing the perpetrator was still fully functional, apparently.

I expected the next volley by the Bishop and it was the easiest lob to return.

"There is concern about the health of your marriage," relays the Bishop.

That my marriage was in trouble was certainly an understatement. It had been apparent to many that there was something askew from the first day we arrived. We held it together as long as we could, but the mortar eventually began to crumble. The Bishop's solution was to recommend more marriage counselling; one must save one's marriage at all costs. However, the more Beth and I went to counselling, the more it accentuated the conflicts. The harder we tried, the worse it got.

Eventually, it became impossible to deny the reality any longer. Home life became rife with verbal assaults. The conflict was inciting viciousness on both sides, with the children either forgotten in the turmoil or caught up in the middle. They became the token treasure that was fought over almost daily. One-to-one time with Andrew and Amelia was the opportunity time for the other party to settle differences. On one occasion I countered this harassment by picking up a broom and swinging it at Beth. It splintered against a door frame.

"Kruk!" squawks Raven. "Is this really worth doing jail time for assault and battery? I suggest it is time we take stalk of the situation and plan an exit strategy."

"You can't just walk away from a marriage," Foxy counters. "What God has joined together let no one rend asunder," quoting the well-worn Bible passage.

That was definitely my quandary. Being a good Bible-believing Christian, I desperately wanted to stay married. There was no way in Fundamentalist Christianity to justify divorce. Marriage is a lifetime commitment. Certainly, more enlightened spiritual teachers could have nuanced these teachings and brought some common sense to bear on my situation. But they weren't in my corner. My faith was a well-buttressed fortress against such liberal revisionism. (This only served to make the most courageous and healthy decisions of my life even more difficult and painful.)

So here Beth and I were, at the point of payback. We had invested fifteen years of our lives to get to this point of raising a young family in a postcard community, with me fulfilling my dream to be a pastor and Beth a stay-at-home pastor's wife. What was missing? Why couldn't we get it to work? If only I prayed harder.

"Yes, I agree. Our marriage is in rough shape," I reply. At least I could be forthright about this.

"Do you agree to continue to go for more counselling?"

"Can't hurt?" I concede with muted enthusiasm.

The litany continues.

"There is considerable concern that your commitment to Lutheran teachings is being compromised by New Age influences," the Bishop states, dead-pan.

In the big wide world outside the fold of conservative Christianity, to be labelled New Age would not necessarily be interpreted as slander. It might even be considered a compliment, as if one were progressive and modern in one's thinking. But this was not the big wide world. It was a small-town outpost, a bulwark against modernity. This allegation was presented as if I was involved in some sort of a cult activity with naked dancing under the moonlight around a boiling cauldron of chicken entrails and bat's wings.

"The naked dancing has its appeal," adds Monkey. "The chicken entrails, not so much."

The principal offence caused by the New Age seems to be the message of human potential. This strikes at the heart for Reformation and Lutheran theology, for which the foundational question was: "How can I make peace with an angry God?" Answer: "Plead the merits of our Lord and Saviour Jesus Christ." For the New Age, the pressing question is: "How can I maximize my potential and become all I am meant to be?" A corollary to this question is: "How do I shake off this Christian hangover of shame, fear and self-doubt?" In many ways, the New Age is a reaction to Christianity's acrimonious representation of humanity's relationship with the

Divine. There is a contrary emphasis on a positive, life-affirming God with no fear of judgement or of being sent to hell. Imagine.

It is a bit of a misrepresentation to speak of the New Age as if it represents a coherent system of thought. There are, however, some generalizations that it might be fair to make. A foundational teaching is that we all have the potential to share in Christ-con-sciousness or divinity. Everyone is a channel of divine inspiration. We all are responsible for our own life path, with no end of avenues to explore: astrology, meditation, aromatherapy, tarot readings, numerology, séances, talking to trees, angels, dream-work, chan-nelling spirits. The emphasis is intensely individualistic, focusing on personal growth and self-fulfilment, often to the exclusion of social or communal responsibilities and interdependence. As we are each responsible for our station in life, in the end we get what we deserve, or at very least, what we have visualized. This can quickly degenerate into a self-indulgent materialistic potpourri, promising whatever your little hedonistic heart desires.

Despite the pitfalls of this often self-serving blend of spiri-tualism and materialism, there was much that appealed to me as a corrective to the life-denying negativity of my Christian roots. According to New Age teaching, each of us has the responsibility and ability to determine what is truth for us. This of course leads to anarchy without checks and balances but, in the words of Raven, a little independent thought was well overdue. I needed to gain a sense of my personal integrity and inner wisdom.

ADULTERY

*Everybody's got something to hide
except for me and my monkey.*

The Beatles, *White Album*

The Bishop's eyes fall back to the letter. There is a seemingly interminable pause before reading the last accusation. With due solemnity, he shifts in his chair again and uncrosses his legs.

"The evidence seems to be mounting that you are having an affair."

So here we are, back to the beginning. What to say? Should I come clean and admit to everything? Should I deflect the accusation and bemoan my dysfunctional marriage?

"Well, we haven't slept together, if that's what you are implying," I mutter lamely. I had clung to this as the criteria of my faithfulness to my calling and to my marriage.

"Now where have we heard that defence before? A little *Clintonesque*, wouldn't you say?" adds Foxy. "Not terribly original and precious little integrity."

Foxy is right. My adherence to social propriety had begun unravelling in serious fashion over the last year. I had committed enough offences to give the Bishop legitimate cause for removing me from the parish.

Monkey breaks into a parody of an old gospel hymn: "He touched her. Oooh, he touched her!"

"Can't you treat anything seriously?" scolds Foxy.

"You are missing the point," counters Raven. Directing his comments to me: "The real offence is that you are in love with someone other than your wife. The time has come for you to make a choice between the ministry, the town and your marriage, or your relationship with Maggie."

"How can I do that?" I despair. "Everything I have believed in, worked for, has all led me to this place. I can't undo my ordination. I can't undo my marriage vows. Those were lifetime decisions. Those vows are made in heaven. I have no part of me left to will a different life."

"True, but this is not about your will but your heart. This is love. Your will and reason are bound by your religious convictions. Your heart, on the other hand, is still wild and free, unclaimed, unfettered, truly a force with which to be reckoned."

A line had stuck from *The Thorn Birds*, which was running on TV at the time, the drama about a Catholic cardinal who agonized over the conflict between his priestly vows and his unconsummated love with a woman. His dying words to his mistress were, "In my life I have had two loves, the church and you, and I have loved neither well." I determined that that would not be my epitaph. A decision was inescapable.

Foxy cuts me off abruptly: "I can't believe how you have to make a big melodrama out of everything! First you are Jesus, now you are Richard Chamberlain. If you had just shown a little discretion, but no, you had to drive out every second day down that long dirt road to their farm, the dust hanging in the air for hours, like a banner in tow – "I am off to visit Maggie!"

"I didn't want to be sneaking around," I reply in defence. "I was trying to be honest."

"Honest? Well then, here is our opportunity," Foxy retorts, wheezing out all the sarcasm he can.

Raven is flapping his wings: "This is exactly what we have been waiting for. Launch out into a brave new world."

I look over to the Bishop as he delicately folds up the letter like *origami*, careful not to make eye contact. No doubt he would be very willing to assist with the launching.

It was time for sentencing. What is my plea? I sit silent and still. Filling the void, the Bishop finally asks, "Will you recommit to your marriage vows?"

"I'll give it a go."

"Do you pledge faithfulness to the Lutheran Catechism and the Augsburg Confessions?"

"The whole thing?" I respond, a bit perplexed. "I guess."

Neither of us take much encouragement from my responses. Apparently I am saying just enough of the right things to buy a temporary stay of proceedings. The Bishop, perhaps confused and disappointed, no doubt frustrated, unclasps his hands, excuses himself, gathers up his coat and heads out the front door. I stay seated until I hear the sound of the car wheels recede down the driveway.

Returning home, awaiting me on the kitchen table is a letter from Gwen. She had written in response to my note about having drawn the H Rune from Norse mythology. Her comments:

> It is interesting that you picked that rune as I consider that my life rune. I see my life work as creating disruption. Of course, disruption is not necessarily a bad thing as much of what gets dislodged needed to be. We do seem to place a negative connotation on disruption, as if only the good stuff will get disrupted! … Good thing you are pure potential or you could never survive this massive transformation. How I enjoy the sight. Love, Gwen.

At least someone is finding this entertaining. Have it your way, Gwen.

TRAP DOOR

*And whether or not it is clear to you now, no doubt
the universe is unfolding as it should.*

Max Ehrmann, *Desiderata*

A few weeks passed, maybe months. Tensions in the community and my marriage were rising, not diminishing. How was I to extricate myself from this mess? I wasn't prepared to abandon my relationship with Maggie. Marriage counselling was just making our home situation worse. The community was, with just cause, losing patience with my lifestyle choices.

At wit's end, I retreated to the cistern in the basement, which I had redesigned months earlier to serve as a sort of retreat centre for just such an occasion. The cistern itself was about six feet cubed, just high enough to stand up in, dusty, dirty and dark, not immediately presenting itself as the type of place where anyone would want to spend time. But my imagination had taken over. I had cleaned out the cobwebs, washed the walls and covered them with cedar planks, which brought appealing visual and scent appeal. I added some candle holders gifted by friends, hung special readings and artwork, laid a foam mat on the floor and covered it with an ornamental blanket.

There were many magical peculiarities of this little cubby-hole that brought encouragement when I needed it most. The entrance was through a small closet door in the basement, with a crawl hole opening through the concrete foundation. Walking through closet doors into a fantasy world was straight out of the Narnia Tales! And climbing through the concrete hole was like entering Jesus' tomb. Inside, because there were no air currents, when I would light the incense or candles I could watch the smoke curl up in the most enchanting patterns. There was also a water pipe in the middle of the floor that went down into the well. I would drop pieces of wax down the old well pipe and send them on their way with prayers. The wax would tinkle, sometimes close to a minute, like fingers running lightly over the strings of a harp. Everything I dropped down this prayer shaft, even leaves, would create this magical tinkling cascade. This process never ceased to fascinate. It always seemed a miracle to me and an affirmation and assurance that I was in a safe and blessed space. And this was definitely a time for a miracle.

As I attended to the stillness of this concrete shelter, the answer was whispered into my ear: "Resign." Resign? Brilliant! Why had it never occurred to me before? The solution was so simple, so obvious. I could get out of this cesspool. Instantly, the confusion and anxiety disappeared. I left my prayer time refreshed and went upstairs to call the church president.

Before I had time to build up the nerve to dial, the President of the Congregation called me. "We have to talk," he said. My problematic behaviour had gone too far and something had to be done. Council was going to have to put its collective foot down.

"No problem. I have decided to quit."

There was a faint sigh of relief from the other end of the phone. "I was expecting as much," he said.

I met that Wednesday evening with the church council and offered my resignation. The council very graciously was open to consider other options, but was not sure anything could salvage my ministry at that point. Resigning seemed to be the most reasonable and dignified option. They were certainly being more than considerate and supportive in this crisis of my creating. We agreed that I could have a few months to allow some space to sort out my affairs, find employment and another residence. It was to be a very gentle and orderly transition. Not.

The Bishop was notified on Thursday. He cancelled all his scheduled engagements for the following day and bee-lined down to our little community. This was now priority church business.

He again met with me privately in the prayer room in the narthex. The Bishop sat with his back to the door. In between us was the small corner table delicately covered with the brocade lace doily and the calligraphied Bible opened to the twenty-third Psalm: "Yea, though I walk through the valley of the shadow of death..."

My imaginary companions are also present. They wouldn't miss such an occasion even if I had insisted on it, which I had. Raven is back on the candelabras, his favourite perch. The sun coming in from the window behind drags his shadow across the wainscoting, giving it an ominous and grotesque distortion every time he turned. There is somewhat of an oracle element to the shadows, reminding me of my tree divination and making me squirm with discomfort. Foxy is curled up on the cushion of the Catholic kneeler, twisting restlessly, desperately trying to get comfortable. Monkey is hanging from the door behind the Bishop, making obscene gestures at particularly inappropriate moments.

There was little discussion. Both of us seemed incapable of addressing the situation directly. The Bishop confirmed my intention to resign. This seemed to be sufficient admission of guilt of whatever allegations might have been brought against me. I certainly felt guilt and shame enough to support that assumption. The Bishop asked what my intentions were. I explained that I planned to step down in a few months and then would like a year's leave from the parish ministry to sort out my personal life.

Nice try. "No can do," replied the Bishop. A pastor had made a similar request before and it had ended up in a nasty lawsuit. Go figure. Very complicated and confusing, this church business. Also, as Bishop he was responsible for my behaviour if I remained on the clergy roster; he couldn't count on me behaving. A safe bet.

He advised me of my options, neither of them involving anything approximating a smooth transition. I had two choices: Door #1: have my name temporarily removed from the roster and undergo an investigation by the ethics committee; Door #2: resign permanently from the roster and avoid any further humiliation. In either case, my resignation would be effective immediately and a vacancy pastor would be in the pulpit for Sunday's service.

I was dumbfounded. I sat paralyzed in my chair, head hanging, eyes focused on the paisley pattern of the red industrial carpet under my feet.

"So what is your decision?" the Bishop asked, keeping focus on the matter at hand. Decisions didn't exactly seem like the most fitting word under the circumstances.

If I had had a little presence of mind, I would have asked for time to take counsel. However, I was not offered that consideration and I did not feel empowered enough to ask for it. I simply complied with what was being directed. Door #1 meant several more months of humiliation for me and everyone in the community. Door #2 offered the hope of getting out of this mess as quickly as possible.

"Just let me resign," I conceded, demoralized. I was convinced it was the Bishop's good graces which were giving me the freedom to escape so mercifully.

Door #2 it was. We proceeded immediately into the church office. I was directed to sit down and write a letter stating that I was resigning of my own free will and was agreeing to have my name removed from the clergy roster. I was also instructed to add that I would not seek reinstatement for three to five years – the old *don't-call-us-we'll-call-you* routine.

A quick scrawl of my signature on the bottom of the page and it was done. I was officially persona non grata. Home, career, identity, community, income – gone! Out onto the street. The church to that point had been my caretaker, my provider, my extended family, my spiritual authority, my safe place. No longer. There was to be no running back to *Big Mother* and begging for mercy. The umbilical cord had been snipped and knotted.

My three companions sit in shock. Foxy is mortified, looking like he had been cornered by a dozen hounds. "I guess we got what we asked for," he mutters sullenly.

"Indeed," chortles Raven with considerably more defiance in his demeanour.

Monkey hangs over the communion rail outside the office with his butt sticking up, taunting, "Spank the monkey! Spank the monkey!"

News of my defrocking spread quickly. That Saturday was some sort of summer festival. The town was crawling with visitors. For whatever reason, I felt that it was necessary to make an appearance at this social function. Mostly mercifully, I was ignored. A few caring folks came over to address Beth and me directly. Stewart and Gertrude, stalwarts of the congregation and community and two of our principal boosters over the years, shared their distress.

"Pastors come and go," said I, in a deflective greeting.

"Yes, but usually with a bit more dignity," Gertrude countered.

Indeed. This trap-door exit offered no end of grist for the rumour mill. As one deacon stated, to be as sexually promiscuous as I was made out to be, I would have had to have been Superman. I even got a call from former parishioners in Regina to check out the story circulating in my former congregation that I had been guilty of child molesting. Nice of them to call. I explained that any offences were more of the adult variety.

Those closer to home made the more reasonable assumption

that I had been caught in bed with Maggie. Why else would the Bishop have acted so incisively?

One particularly colourful story surfaced at the Co-op with me making out with Maggie in the back of my station wagon on the previous weekend down a dead-end dirt road. A friend, overhearing the yarn, commented that that was unlikely since Maggie was in Toronto that weekend.

"Well then, it must have been Pastor banging someone else," he countered.

"Pastor was out of town too," she added.

After a brief pause, the raconteur adjusted his story: "I must have the wrong weekend."

Sunday followed, June 21st, Summer Solstice, with the church full for the first time since Easter. Maggie fortunately was out of town for the week and so avoided much of the head-on from this blow-up. Beth and I and children sat in the congregation while a substitute pastor led the service. After the service, I read my letter of resignation, with my predictable tears. My daughter, three, loyal to a fault, ran up to stand alongside in support.

The congregational president followed with his perfunctory report. He and his wife had been very supportive through this drama, attempting to make interventions at critical times. But now was not the time for sentimentality. The die had been cast. The business of the church needed to be given priority.

Other congregational members made comments. Some expressed their heartbreak, others their confusion, or disillusionment or disgust. One mother, who had her son in confirmation, confronted me in very sincere distress: "How am I supposed to explain this to my son?" I had no idea. I couldn't explain it to my children either. I couldn't explain it to myself.

The congregation eventually filed out. Beth, the children and I were left standing alone in the sanctuary.

THE DAY OF RECKONING

The path of awareness and awakening is full of twists, turns, backtracking, rest-stops, and steep grades, all appearing in no particular order.... The only quality you need is a tiny bit of willingness. The only action you need to take is to lift your foot and take the next step.

William Martin, *A Path and a Practice.*

For many years after being removed from the parish, I wished I had chosen Door #1 and had everything out in the open. I dreamed of some sort of resolution that would have washed away the humiliation and restored my sense of dignity, sort of a *Truth and Reconciliation* process. I had the assumption that if I confessed to all my transgressions with explanations and rationalizations, somehow this would make things right. I did write the congregation on a few occasions requesting further dialogue, but no response.

Just as well. It was presumptuous to assume that the rationale for my choices would have cleaned up any of the mess. (It was presumptuous to think there was a rationale.) There is fiduciary bond between a pastor and a congregation. As preposterous or flagrantly paternalistic as it might seem, I was entrusted with the care of souls. I was to be a model of virtue, the authority on all matters of faith, the purveyor of mercy and forgiveness, the mediator of the Divine presence in the *Word and Sacrament*. I was invited into homes and private lives under the assumption that I could be trusted to bring healing and understanding.

Onto these relationships of trust I had slopped my confusion and duplicity. The values and beliefs that I had solemnly vowed to uphold I was now actively undermining – on their *dime*. The sense of betrayal, the division in the community, the humiliation for those who defended my integrity beyond all rational limits, had settled in deeply. There would be no going back to smooth things over, attempting to put salve on old wounds.

In any event, it wasn't entirely my story to tell. It involved family and friends and congregational members who had no interest in my representing them in a public confession.

As for Maggie telling her story, no one ever asked. Conjectures seemed to have been adequate.

I made one pass at reconnecting with my former ministerial colleagues. Allowance was made for me to speak to the Lutheran ministerial, a privilege not normally allowed to a non-pastor. I am not sure what I hoped for, except perhaps to be understood on my terms about the issues that deeply impacted me – the state of my personal life, my spiritual yearning and learning.

An unrealistic expectation. My agenda did not match the concerns of my audience. The principal point of interest to the ministerial was: "Is the church going to have another embarrassing sex scandal and potential lawsuit on its hands." (We had several of them running concurrently at the time.) I refused to address the issue directly. In my mind, those issues were secondary.

Certainly a few members of the clergy and congregation made efforts in the months that passed to make contact, to express concern about my well-being, to show more caring than I dared to expect. The Bishop wrote me a letter, expressing his heartfelt regret at how things had unfolded. Most of these sentiments were relayed to me second-hand, as I wasn't around to hear. By this time, Foxy and I had headed to the hills, tail between the legs.

For a long time, I searched for someone or something to blame for my calamities: the church, the Bishop, my marriage. Eventually, I grew to appreciate that this was my story and there was no one other than myself responsible for it. This adjustment of focus allowed me to look back with much less judgement and anger toward the incidents and individuals which had disrupted my carefully crafted life of piety. The principal characters with whom my path had intersected – Beth, Maggie, the Bishop – each had their own dramas to act out for their own reasons. If we climbed over each other in our mad scramble to escape self-made prisons, who was to fault? The Bishop, for one, dispatched his ecclesiastical responsibilities with incisiveness and proficiency. It just so happened that this involved dispatching me. Nothing personal.

As it turned out, forgiving others was much easier than forgiving myself. Call it idealism or egotism, I had inflated expectations of myself – to not screw up, for instance. I had plotted a life course that was to allow me to soar above my less-than-dignified beginnings. How did it come about that I landed in the most muddled, compromised situation I could have imagined, and mostly of my own making?

"Talk this one through with me, guys. Was my personal process worth the pain and disruption that it caused?"

"How could you be so arrogant as to even pose such a question?" rages Foxy. "You were once a dignified defender of the faith. This is how you repay the trust that was vested in you?

"Oh, get over yourself, will you?" chides Raven. "Everyone else has. Your ego got a little bruised, that's all. What did you expect? There is a little fallout with every difficult decision; otherwise it wouldn't be difficult. For once you had the guts to take a stand and you are shaming yourself for it? The only shameful part is it took you so long to do it."

Right again, Raven. I had to admit that the choices that caused the most disruption were, in the long run, the most courageous and healthy. When I acted out of the depth of my humanity, however wounded or fearful, I came closest to being the authentic, caring and loving human being that I desired to be.

I apparently had to learn this lesson the hard way in order to learn it well: *If I am not honouring myself at a deep inner level, I cannot trust myself to act responsibly in my personal or public life.* If the resignation process had not been so brutal and incisive, I likely would have missed the learning and taken my act down the road to another congregation. As it was, that lesson was too costly and painful to waste. A big thanks is owed to all those who pushed me to this breaking point.

♩ TANGO INTERLUDE

My learning in tango at this stage, in addition to the mind-boggling intricacies of the steps themselves, is three-fold: how to walk with presence and posture (chest out, shoulders back), how to boldly embrace my dance partner, and finally, how to own the lead.

As it turns out, I am far too polite to be a *tangero*. Being a New Age gentleman (and a bit of a *mommie's boy*), I have learned to be overly sensitive to the woman's feelings and get permission or approval before any sort of joint activity is plotted (sort of a "lead by consensus.") Apparently I have been dancing all this time out of a co-dependent relationship model, paralyzed because I am not willing to risk offence or take responsibility for the dance. Translated into dance form, I will give a little hint at a lead and then pull back to see if my partner understands, approves and chooses to respond in an appropriate manner. If her step is in keeping with my intention, then I can risk taking another step in the same general direction. If not, then we shuffle back to Square One, stuck in a stalemate, two people leaning on each other, neither being decisive, both waiting for the other to act.

My partner cries out in desperation: "More chest!" meaning: "Be definite, bold. Give me a lead I can understand." With the assumed machismo of Al Pacino in *Scent of a Woman*, I prance boldly onto the dance floor, chest out, back straight, confronting head-on the myth that physical contact of any sort is a sexual advance and the equivalent of marital infidelity. I present myself to my partner, filtering through the self-talk that tags me as abusive or manipulative. I accept that a strong lead is not only essential to the dance but actually pleasing to the woman, who responds by showing signs of trust like a head on the shoulder or tighter embrace.

CULTS

The Great Religions are the ships.
The poets are the lifeboats.
Every sane person I know has jumped overboard.

The Gift: Poems by Hafiz

Now began the long, lonely journey toward being ordinary and inconsequential. This didn't sit well with my piously cultivated persona. Call it an occupational hazard, a *messiah complex*, it was easy to become addicted to the ego strokes of being a pastor. My identity and self-respect were enmeshed with being at the centre of a community where everything I did and thought – good, bad or ugly – was of consequence. Even my personality apparently reflected something of the immortal nature of God. People would come away from Sunday Service saying things like, "The pastor seemed like a nice fellow, a regular sort of guy. He even had a sense of humour," as if this had some divine significance. (To be fair, it does take supernatural ability to maintain a sense of humour in the pastorate where a typical joke is a typo in the church bulletin.)

Once on the outside, in the big wide world, no one cared a whit about my opinions or my indiscretions or heresies. It was presumed that no one had the right to dictate another person's behaviour. One was entitled to a private life, healthy or otherwise, without someone looking over one's shoulder or peering in through the bedroom window. In time, after my ego recovered, this all seemed so natural and liberating.

There now remained the challenge of addressing the question: "How did I get myself into this mental vice in the first place?" My research suggested a connection between religious abuse and cultism and my beloved fundamentalist Christianity.

What were they talking about? *Cult* was a word reserved for the other guys, the bad people who believed differently than I did and who were going to hell. This interpretation of cult did not focus on theological correctness but rather on the psychological and sociological health or disease fostered by community dynamics and teachings; a cult was any faith-based community that was manipulative, constricting, and controlling, regardless of creed.

One of the principal manipulative strategies of cults is to cultivate low self-esteem among its members. This makes it easier for the member to submit to the leader's judgements and more difficult to challenge authority. Mistrust of self, submission to authority, censorship by the community and God, strict adherence to the dictates of a charismatic leader and a sacred text with a strict moral code are all such control techniques. Cult adherents reflect a deep desire to have someone else responsible for their life, someone else to make the decisions, call the shots, and determine right from wrong; cult leaders are, of course, happy to oblige.

The payback of such conformity is a strong sense of inclusion and exclusion. Communal interdependence is dependent upon the successful demonization of the outside world. Cult adherents live in an us-versus-them world. The true believers are God's chosen few. Every one of differing beliefs and behaviours are outside of the pale of salvation. There is an externalization of evil, projecting it onto nonbelievers and the Devil. Those on the inside have exclusive claim on the truth and are especially favoured of God. All other religions and differing philosophies are ploys of the Devil to trick one into hell.

Contrarily, my reading in the sociology and psychology of religion presumed that a healthy belief system would foster high self-esteem, personal responsibility, moral autonomy, intellectual integrity, a robust sexual and emotional life, diversity and creativity, and so on. Excuse me? When did my fundamentalist faith ever encourage me to be broadminded and accepting of people whose beliefs differed from mine? When did it foster anything but low self-esteem and a shame-based self-image? When did it empower me with a sense of personal autonomy and respect for boundaries, or encourage a healthy engagement of my sensuality and sexuality, with a valuing of intimacy and emotional connection, or validate my intuition and personal judgement? To the contrary, it cultivated a type of psychological and intellectual dwarfism, nurtured in ghetto communities, buttressed by ignorance and bigotry.

Strangely enough, this type of thinking did have its appeal when I had made my commitment of faith many years earlier. There are particular elements of adolescent psychology that adapt well to the profile of a cult adherent. The complexities of life can seem overwhelming. There is a desire for black and white moral guidelines and unquestionable answers that make the world comprehensible and assist in simplified decision-making. Insecurity about identity is assuaged by belonging to a strong cohesive community with clearly defined boundaries and rites of inclusion.

With advancing years, one is able to work with the ambiguities and make peace with a world of greys. The unquestionable answers surrender ground to the unanswerable questions. One gains an appreciation for the commonality of humanity and the similarities among religions and cultures, rather than the differences. One gathers insight into the duplicity of human nature and the good and evil in each of us, cultivating a distaste for simplistic explanations about life and behaviour, and a mistrust in anyone who makes claims to absolute truth.

Not that this transition into a more expansive faith was necessarily welcome or comfortable. I stubbornly resisted assuming

responsibility for my life's course as long as I could and made repeated attempts to hand over decision-making to someone else: my
parents, the church, the Bible.

The sticky point was, at the end of the day, there was no one
other than me to determine the line my life journey was to take. It
all comes back to walking the path alone, plodding blindly off into
the fog. As painful and confusing as this was, I was nonetheless
reclaiming personal authority, one faltering step at a time.

LETTING GO

There is a moment, a stitch in time
When leaving home is the lesser crime.
Though your eyes are filled with tears
Your heart can see
Another life, another galaxy.

Paul Simon, *Surprises*.

For all the attention that it received, my *falling out* with the church did not *hold a candle* to the emotional trauma of abandoning my children. *Abandoning* is likely not a fair representation of my actions, but that is certainly how I experienced them. Looking on from the outside, one might adopt a much softer judgement; I often received praise for my continued dedication to my children and parenting. But I was not on the outside. I was smack dab in the middle and, my best intentions aside, I felt I was betraying the most sacred trust of a father caring for his children. Nothing was more important. I wanted to protect Andrew and Amelia from every pain and disappointment, stand beside them in every trial, share their every joy. I wanted to be for them what I would have wanted my father to be for me. Now I was walking away from those dreams and ideals.

Gratefully, Beth and I did not have any custody disputes in the early years. I was welcome to come out and spend time as I was able, which was at least three or four times a week in very unreliable automobiles and unpredictable weather. Every evening when I arrived, Amelia and Andrew's faces would be pressed against the window awaiting my arrival. They would bounce into my arms with an intense exchange of hugs and emotions. Then followed fun frenzy: building cardboard forts in the basement or tree houses and snow forts in the back yard, tobogganing, wrestling, skating, riding our bikes to the corner store for candy, garage sales. It was the typical Disneyland Dad scenario (if you can envision being holed up in a basement in rural Alberta as Disneyland), where everything is wonderful for two days and at a pace that no parent could maintain for the entire week. There were a couple of patterns that emerged through all this: time with Dad was to be intense fun, and Dad was always late.

Every night before I left, I would tuck them into bed, which included rituals of reading stories and lying with them. Andrew would cry unless I lay with him until he fell asleep. One night when he was particularly distressed, I had to sleep over and walk him to school the next day. He was crying going to sleep and crying the next morning going to school, not wanting to be left alone. It is a gift of grace that I have ever forgiven myself the disruption that I brought to their precious, delicate, little lives, although it took me the better part of a decade to do so. In the interim, much of my parenting was spent buying affection as an attempt to assuage my guilt. This is not a recommended model of parenting, of course (text books call this *over-functioning* or *agency*), but it got the kids lots of extra stuff. For them, it had the life-long effect of confusing junk food with affection, along the lines of: "Don't cry. Have some more candy."

The key to getting through this upheaval turned out to be allowing myself to fully feel the grief whenever it surfaced. Which made for a whole lot of crying. Often, driving back into Calgary from the kid's place, I would break down in convulsions and have to pull off to the side of the road, unable to drive. A safe thing to do for the most part, with one exception. Late one night, I was pulled off onto the shoulder, engaged in my tearful heaves. I put on my four-way flashers which only worked intermittently. A vehicle coming up from behind rear-ended me at about 70 clicks. I had the car in neutral so that when my car was hit, it was propelled down the ditch for about 30 metres. If it had been in park, I wouldn't be telling this story.

My first reaction to being hit was a calmness and stillness which I instinctively attributed to the presence of angels. After a few minutes passed, I did an internal check: no pain, apparently, no obvious injuries. The front windshield was shattered, with glass everywhere except on me. Apparently, I had been thoroughly blanketed by the angels. The doors were jammed shut, so I climbed out the front window. Once outside, I had a moment to stand in bewilderment, trying to get my head around what had just transpired. I assessed the condition of the car. My recently acquired mid-sized Chrysler LeBaron had been remodelled as a sub-compact, with the trunk compressed up to the back of the front seat.

A police car was by within minutes, and shortly after that an ambulance came to take the other persons to the hospital. I was fine except for a bit of shock. When the cop examined the scene, he suggested that I might consider going to church out of gratitude for being alive.

So there it was: collision, loss, pain, shock and trauma, a perfect metaphor for my life process at the time. Somehow, I came through the thick of it protected. Heartfelt gratitude was certainly an appropriate response, although I wasn't yet up to the challenge of going to church.

Despite all the above, I settled on a very bizarre assertion: however desperate or disruptive, leaving my marriage was a courageous and crucial decision. To stay behind in a non-nurturing relationship for fear of upsetting the children, in the long term would have resulted in more scarring than from the separation itself. To loosely quote Carl Jung, "One of the most destructive gifts to pass on to a child is the unlived life of the parent." To not have chosen to leave my marriage and the ministry, however painful those decisions were, would have resulted in a slow death for all concerned. The consequence of that traumatic, terrifying process was the creation of an expansive, soul-affirming future for myself and my children at very least, and perhaps for others as well. Reversing that process was unthinkable.

Two stories about my children's inner strength stand out in my mind as reinforcement of my choice to create space for them. I took Andrew and Amelia, as preschoolers, on an outing to Fort Calgary. True to the model of the Old West, gophers had overtaken the grounds outside the fort. Andrew and Amelia instantly assumed their characteristic roles in playing. Amelia had the inspiration to catch a gopher for a pet. Andrew, the technician, was responsible for engineering this feat. They found a piece of string and tied a little noose in it and then hung it in front of the gopher hole to catch the gopher in the noose when it popped up. What were the odds? To make the situation more comical, they were frantically running from one hole to the next as each new gopher surfaced. I hung back, resisting the urge to spare them embarrassment from their impossible quest. After about ten minutes, Andrew jerked up the string with a gopher hanging from the other end! The little fur ball was apparently attracted by the brightly coloured string and bit into it. Andrew pulled it up quickly enough, probably out of fright, so that the gopher didn't have time to let go. This left Andrew frantically swinging the gopher in the air, not knowing what to do with it. Amelia stepped in to the rescue and coddled up the little creature as her new-found pet. She was heartbroken when I eventually insisted that she could not take it home and had to return it to its mother. My learning for the afternoon: don't constrict my children's potential with my limited imagination.

A few years later, Amelia, age 9 and all of 4' 2", came to an

Eskimos football game with my pastor friend Randy and me. After every Edmonton score, they throw out those little *nerf footballs*, and Amelia was determined to get one. We were up in the nosebleeds since Randy liked to smoke cigars, far too high up in the stands for a football to reach us. When the Eskimos were threatening to score, Amelia headed down on her own into the mass of much bigger bodies, all standing up to see the touchdown. That was the last we saw of her for about ten minutes. The Eskies did score and the fireworks blasted and the customary footballs where tossed about. Still no Amelia. I was getting ready to panic when suddenly she popped out through the throng, proudly displaying a green and gold football in her outstretched arm.

"I got one!" she proclaimed. "I had to fight a guy for it, but I got it."

Randy's comment: "That girl isn't going to miss much in life."

OPEN SPACE

But little by little,
As you left their voices behind, …
There was a new voice
Which you slowly
recognized as your own,
That kept you company
As you strode deeper and deeper
Into the wood,
Determined to do
The only thing you could do –
Determined to save the only life you could save.

Mary Oliver, *New and Selected Poems*

Abandoning one's connection to a two-thousand-year-old system of rituals, traditions and values that defined one's being is a long, lonely and difficult journey. Religion plays very well the part of *smother-mother*, tightly swaddling the adult child in the protective papoose. It blesses conformity and compliance and excommunicates those who move beyond parochial confines. As the Church puts it, there are only two options: God's way or the highway.

The motif for refashioning my faith that was presenting itself to me was, on the other hand, unfettered and expansive, creative and fanciful. It was more the calling of an artist than a theologian or philosopher, sifting through belief systems, reflecting, absorbing what seemed relevant and moving on, embracing what was needed for the moment, not as forever. There is required an entirely different set of truth tools than used in the process of formulating religious dogma. There is no more proof-texting from an absolute authority. The wrenches and vice-grips of logic and the hammer of debate, the nails and screws of unquestioning belief that keep things secure and in place, the levels and squares that ensure precise judgements, are all out the window. They are replaced with paintbrushes and kaleidoscopes and sponges and blank canvas and walks in the sand in bare feet.

The term *open space* is an euphemistic attempt to put a positive spin on those periods of one's life where the bottom falls out of everything and you end up free-falling with no promise of a safe landing. Open spaces are rife with chaos and confusion, with no charted path or clear signposts. There is no security, nor are there certainties, limits, or structures: nothing to grab onto when you so desperately need it.

The implied gift of open space is that one not only gets to think outside the box, one gets to live outside the box. With good fortune, you may have a friend or two, maybe even a job or a roof over your head, but don't count on it. I suppose I should have been grateful to have had such a magnificent opportunity to recreate my life. I wasn't.

And things were only going to get worse. When I moved into Calgary, I had hoped that I could at least take my relationship with Maggie with me. In fact, at the time I had it in my mind that that was the reason I had gone through this hell. She was my *one and only*. We were to ride off into the sunset together and live happily ever after. As it turned out, I was to leave that dream in the prairie dust as well. Once I left Little Denmark, my relationship with Maggie soured almost instantly. Seems the main function of our connection, for the time at least, had been to assist each other in *getting out of Dodge*. In Little Denmark we needed each other; we were each other's main support. Once on the outside, our mutual dependency had run its course. Talk about a kick in the gut. I thought I had suffered through all the disillusionment possible.

True to form, I hung on to my sunset dream for several years, until my limited prospects became painfully obvious. I felt totally abandoned. Sure, I kept in contact with Rhonda and a few others, but I was alone on a soul level. There was no one to bail me out, no one to give my life meaning or romance or dignity. Just poor, pitiful me. Needless to say, I was a little depressed. Part of every day was spent in tears. Another part was spent staring blankly at the walls of a bedroom that I had rented, barely big enough for the bed. I had trimmed the base of the bed with all my books in a desperate attempt to shore up whatever self-esteem I could muster.

Gwen again to the rescue. She had taught a very helpful exercise in one of her workshops. The three-step meditation progressed as follows: 1) fashion a prayer; 2) identify the desire expressed in the prayer; 3) shuck off the particular form in which the prayer was expressed and open up to the eternal reality underlying that prayer. According to this process, Maggie was not the core reality of my hopes and dreams. She was merely a physical expression of a deeper desire, after the Platonist notion that life on earth is merely a reflection of the heavenly ideal. Maggie was not the heavenly ideal, as much as I desperately wanted her to be. Apparently no one is.

My challenge was to find out what was at the heart of my love for Maggie and identify it in that substrata of reality where it could never be lost and could be experienced fully and freely.

"Fine time to figure that out," scolds Foxy. "Where does that leave us now? All four of us are crammed into this closet-sized bedroom!"

"This doesn't seem like fun," bemoans Monkey, on a rare occasion agreeing with Foxy. "I've spent too much time in closets already."

"It's not supposed to be fun," blurts Raven. "Didn't you read that bit about open space? This is the brave new world! We get to create it all ourselves for ourselves."

"I hate being alone," Monkey sighs.

"We're not alone. We have each other." offers Raven consolingly, uncharacteristically sensitive. "You have yourself," he adds, directing his comment to me.

"And I have me," I echo.

Strangely enough, I wasn't feeling quite as alone as I thought I should be under the circumstances. Turns out, the love and companionship that I had been seeking all this time was my own. Having everything stripped away, including my persona and social standing, my family, my Maggie, was exactly what I needed to bring me face to face with my Self. It was a homecoming of sorts, the rekindling of an old friendship.

If you leave the church, you leave God. That was the proverbial rule that Foxy and I had lived by. Assumedly, God was left behind in Little Denmark, along with everything else that I treasured. But that too did not seem to play itself out as I had expected. God apparently wasn't so easy to shake. As it turned out, God was the constant through all this transition. In fact, leaving the church became the doorway to a new encounter with Source. In the void, my heart was opening to a deeper and richer experience of Spirit. I belonged to no church. There was no ritualistic process to bridge that unbreachable chasm between God and humanity. But instead of being lost in "a world without hope and without God" as the Good Book predicted, I seemed to be lost in God. It is as if I were in utero, cradled in the womb. The umbilical cord that had been tied to the church now connected me directly to Source.

This was all quite a soul-affirming surprise. As a consequence of abandoning all pretence of goodness and theological correctness, my spirituality was deepening. Go figure! Maybe the church didn't own the rights to God after all. Perhaps I shouldn't have been surprised. Maybe closeness to God or Spirit is not conditional on being or doing anything proper. Perhaps God is everywhere there is an opening, a question, a need, a hurt, a desire.

This shift in my relationship with Spirit could be interpreted as a transition in focus from religion to spirituality, a common modern perspective. In popular culture, religion and spirituality are understood to be contradictory and mutually exclusive. Spirituality is presumed to be a desirable quality, whereas religion is judged as irrelevant or anachronistic and an obstacle to spiritual growth and the expansion of the psyche.

In classical traditions, spirituality is considered a subset of religion and subject to theological doctrines as the devotional practice of the pious and devout believer. One would never presume to be spiritual without also adhering to some faith tradition. The richest streams of wisdom flow from sages who were able to hold these two traditions in dynamic tension. Spirituality is interior and subjective; religion is communal and objective and doctrinally based. In spirituality, God is closer than the air we breathe. In religion, God is the *holy other*, distant and separate, whose presence is mediated thorough sacred ritual and worship. The balancing of personal insight against the communal consensus, the individual experience against the objective/ theological, private prayer against public ritual, creates a generative charge that can sustain not only the individual but civilizations as well as.

It just so happened I was not one of those *sages of the ages*. My personal spiritual agenda continually ran afoul of my religious responsibilities and beliefs. I could not keep them in balance. Apparently there was no alternative to being authentic, no matter how risky or vulnerable that could prove to be.

"I had expected more from you, Foxy," I say with sincere regret.

BURNED AT THE STAKE

If I could gently touch your eye of doubt
And help you raise the lid to sights now hidden,
If I could wrap my arms around your heart
So fearful of the seeing,
If I could help you trust that universe
Around the edges of your ordinary sense
And see the main event, I would.
I would.

Gwendolyn Jansma, *Gwenanna: Her Words.*

My introduction to spiritual community in Calgary came at a medicine wheel retreat at the Stoney First Nations, where I met Pat. Coincidentally, I began talking to her about someone I was to contact when in Calgary. "You must be talking about my husband, Fred." Right she was.

This began a connection with some very special people and lifelong friends. The Sharing Circle met every Sunday and was thoroughly New Agey, with lots of hand-holding and hugging. It sure worked for me. I soaked up all the affirmative touch I could get.

Fred became not only my teacher but also my counsellor. After about three weeks of attending the circle, I went to talk to him personally. He made the comment that since he had known me, he had not yet seen one expression of emotion on my face. It was true. I was travelling incognito. I was so shell-shocked from my recent tour in battle that I had learned not to give away any clues to what I was feeling that could be used by the enemy in reconnaissance.

Pat became my energy therapist. She began practising, soon after I arrived at the group, a process called *Kolaimni*, something similar to *Reiki*. It was as if it were made for me. I spent hours on her table while she practised a form of non-touch therapy, massaging and caressing the inner wounds. The loving vibration soaked deep into my psyche. After each session, we would share our sense of what had transpired. Without having spoken a word during the process, we regularly would come up with a very similar sense of the nature of the work done. One session might be about healing some past abuse memories, another about church, another about opening the heart. The sessions were so intense that often it was a good hour later before I was able to walk straight or navigate myself home.

It was at this community that I also met two dear friends, Michael and Natasha. Michael was not only a fellow visionary; he also became my employer when I needed to get back on my feet financially. Natasha was my companion and mainstay for a year and a half. She supported me in my recovery and provided the nurturing that I craved. She also opened her arms and her home to my children, who needed to see their father in a caring relationship. Andrew and I had set up a train table in the basement. Amelia and Natasha would spend hours upstairs reading together. Natasha had been a teacher and Amelia was taking remedial reading in her early years of school. Then there were the walks along the Bow River or in the park behind her house, where the kids and I made forts and snow jumps. I could go on and on recounting memories, all of them very fond and dear.

After about a year, I felt strong enough to come out of hiding and branch out on my own. The ball got rolling with a half-page write-up in the Calgary Herald on religious and spiritual abuse, which featured my own experience and that of a fellow former pastor and friend. We had been running workshops at the time, which I had dubbed *Burned at the Stake* (reflecting a certain flair for the dramatic). The day of the article, the phone rang all day long, obviously striking a nerve. The next day, Sunday a.m., we had a gathering of about thirty people. This served as the nucleus for a healing circle of those with similar wounds and spiritual interests.

One *Burned* workshop provided the opportunity for connecting with an Aboriginal woman, listening to her tell her experiences about growing up in a residential school, having been taken from her family at the age of six and not being able to talk with her siblings during school hours. One of her brothers was suddenly taken from the school. She asked about his disappearance, but was given some story from the nuns that he was taken to another school. It was only many years later that she learned he had been taken to the hospital sick and that she had been denied the opportunity to visit him during his illness. He had had to die alone. At the end of the workshop, she shared that this gathering was the first time she had not been conscious of a White/Indian distinction. This still touches me as one of the most poignant moments from my sessions.

The workshops on spiritual abuse spawned timeless sharing, a sampling of which are related below (with changes to the names and some of the details to preserve anonymity). The common theme is that religion can be a very hurtful place for a lot of people. The opportunity to share these stories in a non-judgemental context provided the space for healing. Consider the following:

Ted: My life as a pastor has derailed my understanding of who I am as a person. My spiritual life feels like a black hole. At this point in my life, the mere experience of coming in contact with anything Christian seems to put me in a tailspin. I don't want it that way, but I don't seem to be able to correct the imbalance.

Andrew: I had to leave my fundamentalist upbringing when I learned some of the discrepancies in the teachings. But in so doing, I also had to leave behind my family and friends and my social network. My family still doesn't acknowledge me.

Brent: When I started dating, I would wake up in the night

and find my parents praying over me to protect me from "the se-
ductive ways" of my non-Christian girlfriend. They were sure that
I was going to go to hell and had me pretty convinced of it as well.
Those images of them hovering over me still cause nightmares.

Ralph: The church was my life. My father was a pastor. Because my father was so closely identified with the church, I went
to the church to find the love and acceptance which I needed from
my father. It took many years of struggle to realize that the church
was not a substitute for my family. I kept going back to it in an
addictive pattern, expecting something it could not give. That need
led to a drug addiction, which I have only recently been able to
overcome.

Charlotte: At the age of seven I was taken from my reserve, my
home, and taken to a church school, a compound. It was a large
dormitory school surrounded by a high fence. I was not allowed
to leave the compound except perhaps for an evening a week to go
into town to see a movie, if I was good. I was only allowed to return
home during the summer months.

Caroline: I grew up in a fundamentalist town. Every day, when
I went downtown as a little girl, I would be confronted by street
evangelists, preaching that my family and I were all going to hell. I
grew up believing I and my family were evil.

Elizabeth: I can't stand the word "God." All I can think of is
someone angry and mean who is going to punish me. I tried so
hard to get God to love me. I did everything. I went to confession
several times a week as a little child of 10-11, even when there was
nothing to say.

Debra: I used to be part of a very tight-knit fundamentalist
community. At some point, my beliefs stopped making any sense.
Unfortunately, it was an all-or- nothing proposition with that
community, so I had to quit. After that, no one would talk to me.
Old friends would call up to talk to my husband and if they got me

on the phone, they would not even acknowledge me, simply ask for my husband.

Bridgette: I was the only Protestant child in a Catholic school. At the beginning of the school year, the Sister intended to make an example of me. She wrote my name, which she said represented my soul, on the blackboard. At the beginning of each week, she would ask me if I had attended Mass. I would say, "No." Then she would erase a letter of my name. By the end of the term, my soul had been completely erased.

The most life-altering outcome of all this work-shopping was also the most unexpected. Synchronistically, Elaine from Calgary (unknown to me at the time), had picked up one of my brochures out of interest and taken it with her to a *Creative Change Conference* in West Virginia, at which she was presenting. While there, she made acquaintance with a woman from Edmonton, Patricia (also unknown to me at the time), who was attending the conference. In their conversations, Patricia shared her experience of getting expelled from a senior education position in the Catholic Church for being too progressive in her teaching. It struck Elaine that Patricia might be interested in the work I was doing, and so she retrieved the brochure and passed it on to her.

When Patricia returned to Edmonton, she gave me a call to ask if we could perhaps meet to discuss shared insights or experiences. I was excited to do so, and so we scheduled a meeting in Red Deer. On our first meeting, Patricia and I were star-struck. Tears were shared about our parallel grief. There was a comforting hand on the shoulder, conjecture about working together, all in all a much deeper connection that either of us had intended or anticipated.

As the universe continued to unfold, I negotiated a ride to the coast with Patricia, who happened to be going to Seattle for another Creative Change workshop. I was heading out that way as well, to spend some time at my sister's cottage on the idyllic Sechelt Peninsula, north of Vancouver. By the time the trip came around, I was joining Patricia at the conference and she was spending a week with me at the cottage, a week stationed on a cliff's edge, overlooking the stunning Sechelt Bay, eagles soaring up the cliff face in front of the full glass front of the cottage, whimsical arbutus and Queen Anne cherry trees on all sides, seals bellowing from the rocks off the shore. Every morning (but not too early), we were greeted lovingly by my sister and her husband, my brother and his wife and my mother with a fresh supply of crabs, oysters or salmon.

Quite likely you have seen one of those outrageous paintings in a church basement where the heavens are open and the sun's rays are cascading through the clouds and angels descending with harps and cornucopia and anything else required for a good time. This was kind of like that scene.

⚜ TANGO INTERLUDE

Several years of lessons and several other teachers pass through our lives. Beatrix and Michael, itinerant dance instructors, billet with us for a few days while in Edmonton. Their style is *milongero*, the soft, cuddly moves of close embrace, rather than intricate, complicated manoeuvres of salon tango. Close embrace is far less showy, less acrobatic, more subtle, more sensual. Attention is given to making the most out of the least, spending the maximum time possible with the simplest of steps. One dances with a continuous body-to-body awareness of the other, rather than occasionally coming together. It is not feet following feet or chest seeking chest but whole bodies moving together in unison. There is no cat-and-mouse chase, no seduction.

Beatrix teaches *following* with all the elegance of a classically trained ballet dancer. Her leg floats weightlessly on a backward *ocho* without ever losing her centre of balance. Instinctively responsive to the slightest shifts of a man's body, she pleads continually, "Less lead." Definitely no place for this macho man-handling that has become my default style *Giving a lead*, suggests the image of opening a door and inviting the woman to step through, according to Vicente. Tango is the last outpost of good old-fashioned chivalry, apparently.

Michael, a full-time dance instructor for close to forty years, is a master mechanic at assisting his students in adjusting their steps to these subtle techniques. We are informed that the lead of the man, although definite, is very soft. The man must be acutely aware of the positioning of his body in relation to his partner's body at all times. Shifting weight, maintaining one's balance, staying connected, become the main foci of the dance. I learn simple shifts in balance and alignment that make steps, once impossible, now seem natural. I leave the lesson with misty eyes.

EMPTYING THE CLOSET

The Storyteller and the Keeper of Nightmares

The Storyteller keeps the history of our lives. He puts the days of our lives in order and makes sense of them. It allows us to remember. As our lives unfold, the Storyteller keeps up the flow of our thinking, telling the tale as we live it.

But sometimes things happen that are too much for the Storyteller. Sometimes there is no time for talking or even thinking. Some things are too terrible to be put easily into words. At times like this, it is needful for the Storyteller to go to sleep so that we can simply act, in order to survive.

But we do not forget what happens when the Storyteller is asleep, because another part of our mind is fully awake. This part is the Keeper of Nightmares. The Keeper is very strong and quick and smart. Under the guidance of the Keeper, we can do many things. The Keeper will guide us to do whatever we have to do to stay alive. The Keeper does not care much for our history, our family, our beliefs; the Keeper wants only one thing – survival. The Keeper also remembers what happens, but these memories are kept in the form of pictures and sounds and smells, and they are stored in the basket of nightmares.

When we are safe, the Storyteller wakes up, and the Keeper of Nightmares tries to get the Storyteller to hold the memories that it has in its basket. He sends dreams, and nightmares, and feelings, and pictures to the Storyteller. But the Storyteller does not want to accept them as true, because he was not there when these things happened. He tries to send the Keeper and his images away. This struggle leaves the person very confused, and the person may try and drink the struggle away, or stay so busy that there is no time for the struggle, or just pretend that the struggle is not there. The person may feel like they are going crazy; they may not want to talk about the struggle.

But the Keeper is strong and does not give up. One way or another, he will find a way to make the Storyteller accept the memories that he holds. The person can help end the struggle by sitting down with another person or with a group of people, telling the whole truth and reconciling the two parts of the mind.

When we tell our stories, out loud, to a person who cares about us and cares about our struggle, then the Storyteller will listen. And when the story is accepted and placed into the basket of the Storyteller, then the Keeper of the Nightmares can relax and be at peace, and the struggle will end.

Peggy Senger Parsons, David Niyonzima, and the Trauma Healing and Reconciliation Services of Bujumbura, 2003. Used with permission.

Down the hallway from our shared bedroom in the house in the country, blistering hot in the summer and frigid in the winter, was the closet: dark, long, and musky storehouse of memories and treasures. There were chests that held old clothing and costumes saved for Hallowe'en; stacks of *National Geographic* and dusty *Readers Digest Condensed Books*; my father's O-gauge train set; his ivory chess set, from which we borrowed pieces to people our Dinky cars and Tonka trucks; my mother's beaver fur coat and mink shawls. There were family photo albums of trips of all descriptions: fishing and hunting expeditions, reels of 8mm film of sailing from Nova Scotia up the Saint Lawrence Seaway across the Great Lakes to Thunder Bay, at the head of Lake Superior. Newspaper clippings of the journey with our pictures on the front page of the local newspaper.

Mostly the closet remained a mystery. There were dark corners that we never explored, simply because the light did not penetrate. It served as the perfect place to hide Sandy when the monster came to prey.

Through time and troubles, this plaster and wood lathe room, with a 40W light bulb hanging lamely from the ceiling, evolved into an imagined psychic repository for the pain and abuse that sometimes passes for growing up. Storage space for the sobs that were not heard, the stories not acknowledged by those in authority who had the power to change things. To this imaginary closet, my spirit fled for safety during my repetitive nightmares. To this closet, I projected my soul-body when my friend and I were being victimized.

To this closet I needed to return to unpack all the accumulated psychological baggage that had hamstrung me throughout my life: the scars of sexual abuse that robbed me of personal power and healthy sexuality, the unresolved pain and the need to heal, the anxieties and fears that drove me to seek security and refuge in the rigidity of religious fundamentalism. From somewhere deep within, I salvaged the boldness to begin the long, treacherous process of unravelling and exposing, hoping that in confronting these demons they might shape-shift into angels.

Slowly, hesitantly, I stepped back into the reality that I had repressed, kept locked up for several decades. In a trance-like state, I found myself again fumbling at the closet door, hands sweaty and clammy with anxiety, frozen before the void, paralyzed with fear. The door opened. The darkness was consuming, almost suffocating. I gazed in with a mixed sense of attraction and foreboding.

For a long time, there was only emptiness. Then, ever so faintly, arose a soft scuffing, shuffle-step of slippers coming my way from deep inside the closet. I was drawn to the musky body odour that filled the air. A strong, familiar male voice called my name. A hand reached out from the darkness and pulled me to him, body to body, my soft child's face against a man's rough facial stubble. For a moment, I felt special. This was an expression of affection from the face and voice that I loved and trusted. But then it stayed too long and pressed too hard. The affection became smothering and oppressive, something other than I had expected, wanted, or needed. It became difficult for me to breathe. I struggled but was unable to extricate myself.

My therapist used a method called *Integrated Body Psychotherapy*, incorporating bizarre props to assist in body awareness. She invited me to select some pieces of coloured wool from a bowl and to lay these strings together to create a protective circle around me. Simple as this procedure appears, it was excruciatingly difficult. As I picked up the pieces of string, the awareness of someone attacking me sexually was overwhelming. I began to gag and choke and then scream. My face and body twisted into contortions. I tore at my shirt. It was as if a demon was being exorcised. I cried out in my trance, "Dad. Stop!" After five to ten minutes, the convulsing subsided. This evil psychic mass had seemingly been expelled. In its place was a feeling of lightness and pride in my courage to revisit this ordeal and to put the boots to it.

She then led me in a meditation. My mind's eye was drawn away from the scene of the crime to the field outside my childhood home. It was filled with brilliant gold flowers as far as I could see. The vision is so overwhelming that the sense of gratitude displaces the revulsion I am experiencing. Over my shoulder, an angel assures me that, in the midst of the pain and ugliness, there is to be found tremendous wealth and beauty.

The wealth motif followed me home. After paying up at the end of our session, I stopped in on my way at the Instant Teller to replenish my wallet. When I typed in my bank request, it passed me an extra $200! Expectorated like a gob of phlegm. Enough to cover one more therapy session and a cappuccino. Thanks, Bank Machine Angel. I appreciate the encouragement.

The closet overflowed with more memories to reclaim and release. I returned, this time with a sense of anticipation and intrigue. It felt as if something other than terror or trauma awaited. Recollections began to tumble forward, one at a time, and then were almost cascading forth. Smells, sights, touch. My childhood began exploding around me in Technicolor.

The realization hit me that, up to that time, I had had no sensual awareness to accompany my memories. The experience was like someone gaining sight or hearing for the first time. The better part of the next three days were spent laying around my apartment reliving these long-lost memories, revisiting the grand home in the country in which I grew up. Each reminiscence opened like the scented bud of a flower: climbing up the sappy spruce trees, catching lightning bugs in a jar on a dark warm summer evening, the soothing fragrances of the lilacs and apples trees and roses, the roads and ruts in the sandpit, the squeaking of the rickety old swing set, sitting in the hot sun petting our German Shepherd, Sheba.

There still remained huge gaps in what I could recall. The house was always empty. There were no people in it, however hard I tried to visualize them. On one occasion, I had a split-second visualization of my father's face, and I was an emotional wreck for the rest of the day! My bedroom remained an unenvisionable black hole.

I delve deeper into the closet. The door opens more easily, and instead of the darkness, there is a light rose hue emanating, as if from the pre-dawn sun. I reach in tentatively. My fingers begin stroking the head of a large animal, then moved across the bridge of the nose to massage a raspy tongue and large bared teeth. It is the bear rug that covered the living room floor, on which my younger brothers and I romped most every night. Reaching further, my Roy Rogers gun set, my *Jon Gnagy drawing set* that used to keep me company early every morning, when I would go down to the dining room table and practice sketching. And my first pair of skates! And right next to them, crumpled into a ball, my *Bobby Hull Chicago Black Hawks* sweater.

Slowly, piece by piece, my past comes back to me with comfort and warmth. Family is now materializing. My father is taking off his bush boots after a long day of hunting, the fresh smell of the Northwestern Ontario wilderness wafting from his wool sweater. Other smells linger, of trout frying in butter and apple pie and dried birch crackling in the fire-place.

LONG-LOST FRIENDS

And the end of all our exploring
will be to arrive where we started
and know the place for the first time.

T.S. Eliot

... for always night and day
I hear lake water lapping with low sounds by the shore;

– William Butler Yeats, *Innisfree*

Scott and I met in Grade One at McKenzie School, and for the next eight years were inseparable. The O'Malleys lived in an A-frame house on a cliff overhanging Lake Superior, the most dramatic setting imaginable for growing up, steeped in the relentless rhythm of the pounding of the breakers on the rocks below, the oft-times gale-force winds rattling their floor-to-ceiling windows, as if threatening to lift their house off its moorings.

Growing up on the North Shore of Lake Superior evoked an extravagant and unfettered spirit. In front of us was the largest freshwater lake in the world, behind was forest all the way to Hudson's Bay. This entire vista was our playground: swimming, fishing, sailing, hunting, skating, sledding. Up and out first thing in the morning and, except for meals, never coming inside until long past sunset.

We would alternate weekends back and forth at each other's homes, spending our winters sledding and skating and our summers on the water. What we could not do at the one house, we did at the other. Scott and I never missed Saturday morning hockey at the Recreation Centre. Scott played goal. I was a forward. Some mornings, it was so cold there would be hardly enough kids to make a team, but my father would oblige us and take us down anyway, gathering up other neighbourhood kids along the way. Once there, he would start up the old coal oil stove, which was barely warm enough to heat a cup of coffee, let alone frozen feet. None of that mattered. We were Canadian boys in rural Ontario: there had to be hockey!

Then there were the boat trips, sailing on *Cloud Nine*, my father's 45-foot ketch. One trip in particular stands out, heading through the Nipigon Straits on Lake Superior. The water was lukewarm, the waves were fifteen feet high and we got to ride on the bowsprit! Hanging on tenaciously to the stanchions, we would crash down into the next trough, the waves breaking over top of us, lifting us up and threatening to wash us up off the deck. Worth a thousand circus rides! Then sailing out to Sauer's Bay at the head of the Sleeping Giant, getting flattened by the squalls that would funnel down the face of the mountain as we approached the harbour, as if Nanibijo was making one last desperate attempt to protect his treasure.

Scott was the first call I would make on Christmas day, to find out what he had gotten for presents. (I had to wait until 10 a.m. because his parents had been up all Christmas Eve partying.) Scott and Doug got *flubber* one Christmas, which we threw all over their living room, miraculously without breaking anything. Their big vaulted ceiling allowed limitless angles for bouncing and ricocheting. They also got a bongo board, the original balancing board, which also ricocheted all over the living room. Another year they got an Indian rubber ball, which we could pitch from their deck and watch it bounce endlessly over the frozen Lake Superior, 50 feet below. Then we would have to skate out after it. Another Christmas, they got a huge kite to pull you along on the ice. Unfortunately, it was soon after claimed by the cavernous sky and we had to resort again to bed sheets. My gifts always seemed more conventional – hockey equipment, toboggans, clothes, dump trucks.

Scott got the prettiest girlfriends. No wonder. Blue eyes, long blond hair. How did he get to have his hair over his ears like George Harrison when I had to suffer the humiliation of buzz cuts once a month? His social sophistication earned him centre stage in our little country public school. He knew the right things to say, the right clothes to wear. He knew some of the basics of social interaction that it took me another 30 years to figure out, like "girls liked being talked to, not poked or spit at." I was 40 before I determined that smiling at a woman was not a sexual overture!

In later years, Scott introduced me to the right music: Bob Dylan, Led Zeppelin, Janice Joplin, Cream, Isaac Hayes, The Band, Paul Butterfield. We learned from each other's bodies, talked about short skirts and wet dreams, rummaged together through my older brother's Playboys, learned to drink and smoke dope together.

Growing up eventually meant growing apart. Scott moved into the city before I did and continued to specialize in coolness. He went to the *in-school*, and on the weekends he got drunk and smoked up or dropped acid. I was afflicted with a fairly severe case of nerdiness; when I got drunk, I got sick or obnoxious or started crying. When I smoked pot, I turned green. When the drug of choice turned to chemicals, I bowed out.

This wedge in part provided the impetus for me to enter my religious fanatical phase and make the separation complete. I condemned Scott and all my irreligious friends to hell and went on my way.

Now I am holding in my hand a letter from that same friend, crafted in the neatest calligraphic handwriting, the first contact we have had in twenty-five years. He writes: "I have roamed the country experimenting with lots of different lifestyles and experiences, keeping what was important, leaving behind the rest. But there has always been within an ache, an empty hole inside that only you could fill. I am hoping you feel the same and would like to rekindle our friendship."

Truth be told, Scott, I had not given you or anyone else from my pre-Christian days much thought. I erased everything from my mind. How can I communicate that? How can anyone appreciate this survival strategy of amnesia and not hear it as a personal affront?

The letter includes a phone number. I dial with apprehension, my trembling fingers having difficulty hitting the right keys, the empty spaces between the rings seemingly interminable. A boisterous greeting booms from the other end of the phone, "Fred Kruk! No shit!" As I take in the raspy, smoke-stripped voice, something starts to shift inside. The calluses that had built up over the childhood emotions begin to break away and my heart opens to the warmth and faithfulness of a lifelong friend.

I had just signed up for *Facebook*. The same week, my childhood sweetheart, Sandy, signed up 2,000 miles away and then decided to look me up. Forty years later! The snowball was just beginning to roll.

"Fred, I had to track you down. My charming husband of 27 years convinced me that my healing would not be finished until I could thank you for all you did and tried to do for me. Hopefully you have not forgotten your many acts of heroism and what a good and honourable person you are at heart."

What on earth was she talking about? I remember cowering in a corner. That's not what I call heroism. What part am I missing here?

"Do you remember the music box with a ballerina in a tutu dancing so daintily?" said Sandy. "I loved to listen to it, and sometimes when you hid me under the eaves in that closet, you would give it to me so I could play it while I lay there for long hours, hiding. You were so thoughtful! You didn't want me to feel so alone. And every year I hang a toy soldier on my Christmas tree, thinking of you. In my mind, you have always been straight and tall and masterly, and fighting for the right. You appointed yourself my Guardian Angel, my Toy Soldier."

"You used to help me hide. I could hear him threatening you as he searched the house, but you never gave me away. Then there was the attic storage; you would pull the boxes from out of the corner of the closet, I would crawl into the space, then you would pile the boxes in front of me. Don't you remember?"

I remembered nothing, absolutely nothing, other than that night with the creaky ladder at the end of the bed. That, apparently, was enough trauma to fill my childhood consciousness. For 45 years, I had carried the shame for not having been able to defend my prima ballerina.

"Fred, we were children, trapped in a world of adults who were cowards." she counselled. "You were as much a victim as I was. Please don't ever feel that you failed me! The only person who put their life on the line to protect me was you. That is why it was so important to find you again, so I could let you know just how much you made a difference in my survival. You taught me that sexual abuse is not acceptable, and it is not inevitable as I was told. You gave me comfort, you held my hand under the blankets, you squeezed my hand, you let me know that you understood and you felt as helpless as I was. You did not fail me! You were not a coward! You were the bravest person in my world! So Fred, don't ever underestimate the impact you have made upon this world. You are my hero! Don't ever forget it!"

I read and reread her comments, searching for an opening within to draw it inside. My world was rocked. Am I this child hero? What to say?

"Move over Howdy Doody. Back up on the pedestal, Tin Soldier. Let the dancing begin!"

FORGIVING THE DREAM

All your images of winter
I see against your sky.
I understand the wounds
that have not healed in you.
They exist
because God and love
have yet to become real enough
to allow you to forgive
the Dream.

Hafiz: The Gift

With the encouragement of a good friend and therapist, Jonathan, Patricia and I attend a *Family Constellations* workshop. Fascinating format: the facilitator, the counsellee and the other participants band together to dissipate negative force fields, the coagulation of energy that has formed around pain and trauma and that keeps us tied to the past and prevents love from flowing freely. Each participant brings some issue from the past that presents some inhibiting emotional blockage. These scenarios are embodied by members of the group until an energetic breakthrough is realized.

It is now my turn to present a story. I have no intention of saying anything in particular until my stories of childhood abuse begin to surface. In keeping with procedure, I select participants to represent the principal characters in my drama – friends, siblings, parents and grandparents. For the next hour, my trauma is borne by others, to carry, embody and transmute.

I sit passively as a member of the audience, all the while wrenched with rage and humiliation. Awareness of previously unacknowledged abuse surfaces. My face contorts. At intervals throughout the ordeal, the facilitator stares into my eyes to see if I was still present and not at risk of being re-traumatized. I nod to indicate that I am OK and want to proceed. I want to clear this up once and for all.

"I have the distinct awareness that this is not merely about you," the facilitator assesses. "This abuse goes back generations and generations, from your father to his father's father, drawing energy from a culture of pain, suffering, abuse and violence. The work we are doing today will not only benefit you but will also release the souls of your family and countless others who have been entrapped in this web of violence."

She continues to work with the representatives. My childhood girlfriend is curled up in the middle of the floor at the feet of her abuser. He reaches down to touch her. I want to scream, run to her defence, kill the bastard. But his approach is gentle and tender. He no longer has the look of one with aggression or perpetration on his mind. His face is sullen, sorrowful, his cheeks are hollowed, his eyes misty and glazed. He takes her by the hand and invited her to stand. In a tenuous voice he asks, "Will you forgive me?"

I scream inside, "Don't do it. That cock-sucking bastard raped us both!"

But she is unaffected by my silent screams. "I forgive you," she says, gently, softly and sincerely to her assailant. They embrace. Tears of cleansing and absolution flow together.

The energy and focus then shifts to the generations of ancestors also mired in this violence, abuse and aggression. One by one, parents and grandparents are offered up to the Light for the needed healing, cleansing and release, until all are embraced by forgiveness and love.

Later that week, my father comes to me in a dream: "I am giving you back your life, your spirit, which has for so long been enmeshed with your heritage. You have taken into yourself the anxieties, insecurities, complexities, perversions that belonged to

me and to my ancestors. You have borne in your body and your
heart the wounds and burn marks of every touch, every act of betrayal, every misdirected cutting remark of generations prior. These
you may now release. You are no longer trapped in the dance of
abused and abuser, defender or oppressor. They do not need rescu-
ing, nor do you. You are not responsible."

Holding his strong, tanned hand to his mouth, he blows out
across his palm. His soft blue eyes follow his breath to light gently
on me. His mouth closes and forms into a soft smile. In his breath,
he is giving back to me freedom of body and will as if, for the
first time, they both belong entirely to me. I am whole, complete,
self-reliant. I am not responsible for all that was done by others to
others, nor to me.

In the beginning was a childhood notion, the dream that I
could count on the big people in my life, that home would be a
safe haven, that those to whom I looked up and had power over me
would be worthy of my respect and confidence.

How do I make peace with childhood trauma? Previous attempts at forgiving and forgetting merely had the effect of glossing
over rather than confronting the truth and resolving conflict. It
amounted to not much more than simply sweeping the messes
into the closet. And whom do I forgive and for what? Can I draw
an irrefutable link between one person's vice and another's suffering?

Fifty years later and everything and everyone has changed. My
memory is scanty at the best of times. Most of what happened is
still buried in a black hole that is carefully guarded by the Keeper
of the Nightmares. Every once in a while, the Keeper releases a
poltergeist, and then my work of translating a body memory into
intelligible consciousness begins anew. But it has been a long time

since anything has surfaced from that unconscious reserve. Perhaps the well is dry. Not necessarily a bad thing.

And who am I in all of this? The abused victim? A valiant warrior? A complicit bystander? Primary and secondary traumatic stress psychically fused me with each of these roles. For the most part, I played the role of the rescuer, although with limited success. At other times and in other ways, I was also the abused. The scars from those offences affected everything from sexual functioning to relationships to religion. Intimacy was equated with sex, and sex, understood from a power-over dynamic, was rejected as perverse and abusive. I lost a healthy sense of boundaries and personal power that would have empowered me to care for my own interests as well as respect the needs of others, leaving me and others around me, including my children, at risk of further violation and abuse.

But the role confusion did not end there. I also internalized the instincts of a sexual predator, attuned to and aware of opportunities to exert power over vulnerable parties. Although I did not act on these instincts, nonetheless it was often necessary to exert a conscious choice not to do so. When our friends from Regina called to check if I was being accused by the Bishop of child molestation, (one of the few things I was not in fact presumed guilty of), I was not shocked or offended. In some way, it felt like that I was finally found out.

As I sort through the conflicting experiences and outcomes, one conviction seems to hold firm: trust had been betrayed. The dance had been despoiled. The boy soldier had been toppled from his pedestal, robbed of his stature and dignity and his dream of the world as a safe place where gentleness and goodness are respected and where a young child can grow up unscathed.

Perhaps all that remains to be forgiven is the dream.

HOUSE CLEANING

Perhaps we will have to face the darkness, walk out onto the moon alone at nightfall, or dive to the bottom of the sea before the old ossified ego boundaries can be shattered to make room for the dance.

Marion Woodman and Eleanor Dickson, *Dancing in the Flames*

It is a warm summer morning, the entire wild world waiting to be explored, with nothing standing between my two younger brothers and me and the great outdoors other than a messy room.

"You can't go out to play until you clean your room!" echoes my mother's command.

So there we are, wading through clothes and toys strewn about, picking up and putting away, making beds, sweeping floors, when we ached to be outside playing. The whole ordeal is torture, but it has to be. Those are the rules.

Early December. I send Gwen a small package with some local craft items. She writes in response: "On Christmas Eve I had this dream: I see a square room, wood floor, no furniture in it. I look at it from above. As I look three small brooms appear. They are like little whisk brooms with very soft, almost feathery bristles. They sweep – or dance- around the room. I heard this message, "All of your past is being swept clean from the corners of your life." ... I then pick up all my mail and your gift of a small ornamental whisk broom was in it! I could hardly believe my seeing!"

So here I am, with more than half of my life gone, following Gwen's lead, still hard at this *housecleaning of the soul*, wading through a psyche littered with nightmares and trauma and loves lost, finally getting around to finishing the job so I can go out to play.

I dream about a clean room. I am visiting an orphanage in my work capacity as Guardian. There are half a dozen young boys living in a gymnasium - type arrangement, a large open room, totally empty, no furniture or toys. There is an instant bond with this younger child, age four. He strikes me as somewhat simple, in the sense of being innocent and unencumbered with worry or confusion or marring life experience. On his chest is a breastplate, Native American warrior style. We play together very affectionately, just the two of us on this hard gymnasium floor, with no distractions or obstacles. Eventually, the supervisor returns and says it is time for me to leave and for the residents to go to bed. The bed in this case was a large cupboard. Each of the residents had their own drawer in which they slept. I raise my little friend to put him in his shelf. He reminds me very sweetly that I have to turn him over a certain way before I place him on his shelf.

As I am leaving, distraught, sobbing, the supervisor comes over and puts her arm around me. "Are you interested in adopting this boy?" she asks.

"More than anything!" I blurt out, then pause. "But first I have to clean up my life to make a proper space for him."

Back to my analyst. This child of four years old represents my pre-trauma Self, my uncluttered and uncontaminated spirit. Imagine! I had contacted my soul in its innocence and essence! That this existed as a possibility was astounding. He had been kept protected in a closet all the while for me to reclaim when the time was right. Although the living environment resembled institutional confinement, the austerity was more of purity and perfection.

Through the accompanying outpouring of tears, the anger and grief and inner turmoil that had haunted me for the past 50 years dissipated. My spirit no longer felt compromised or conflicted, needing to navigate ever so carefully through minefields of perversion and pain.

The opportunity had presented itself to reclaim what was lost. I had arrived to the point in my life where I was mature and strong enough and gentle and wise enough to create a safe space where my inner child could be loved and cared for. This was real-life time-travel, starting over from the beginning with a clean slate. All that remained was to clear out the clutter and set my house in order.

I receive in the mail a Christmas present, a tree ornament from Sandy, a tiny wood, toy soldier, the same one that she had hung from her tree for the past thirty years, reminding her of my valour in protecting our friendship. It is now entrusted to my care, to encourage me to care for my inner child with that same spirit of courage and diligence that cared for her.

⚜ TANGO INTERLUDE

Over the course of my travels I make contact with another Gwen, a tango instructor from the West Coast, who combines dancing and body awareness and movement with transpersonal psychology. Using the tango dance form as a vehicle, Gwen helps people identify emotional and psychological blocks and reactions related to trust, control and intimacy.

We connect one afternoon in a hole-in-the-wall dance studio in downtown Red Deer. Gwen presents as attractive, middle-aged, svelte and self-confident. This should be fun. We shuffle up the squeaky stairs into the back boiler-room and prepare for our afternoon flight into fantasy.

This is definitely dance instruction with a twist: one part dancing, one part reading, one part writing and in our case, three parts talking. The focus is not on dance moves but rather the dynamics of movement and how this conveys or betrays self-awareness. The sensual and sometimes seamy dynamics of tango present a stage for exploring blocks to trust, communication and intimacy, and issues which extend far beyond the dance floor.

Questions surface: *When is power not power over? When is strength not abusive? When is intimacy not sexual? When is sex not manipulative?* I am now in the privileged position of exploring these issues with someone who not only understands these questions but has done formal training in addressing them through my preferred learning medium.

Gwen introduces her focus: "The body stores every moment of our life – good, bad, joy, trauma - it is with us all the time. However, it is usually the bad and the traumatic that block us, that present resistance to moving with power and joy and allowing us to connect both on the dance floor and in life.

Time to put these theories to the test on the dance floor."

Dance #1. Relatively smooth. No fatal errors. No shins kicked. No feet stepped on. Butterflies exorcised.

Gwen's assessment: "You know a lot of steps and have good musicality. But I felt we were lacking a bit of intensity and connection. You seem to be using your body to protect yourself rather than to express yourself."

"Well, yeah. I am feeling just a little conspicuous. But that is typical me. I prefer to hide."

"Hide from what?"

"Basically a survival instinct. I have had my share of getting beat up, stepped on. Typical childhood routine. I learned early that it was best to keep my head down and stay out of the way."

"And you have internalized that self-consciousness, of course. Loss of presence, power, confidence. So let's look at power issues and developing confidence around being seen." Redirecting me to the mirror, Gwen asks, "What do you see."

"Poor posture, slouching, arms dangling. The limp-rag look."

"So let's try and get some strength into those arms. When you wrap your arm around a woman think of your embrace extending all the way around the both of you as a sort of cradle."

Back to the dance floor to explore the new concept. I do the *power-arm routine* this time, strong, firm.

"Better. Much more strength. But loosen up your grip." Gwen says. "You don't need to hold me tightly. You need to give me a structured space which allows for movement but also provides security." Mental translation: strength does not mean controlling or manhandling. Haven't I heard that somewhere before?

Another dance follows.

"You still seem to be stuck in this polarized image of an all powerful and abusive male on one hand and a powerless, submissive female on the other."

In defence, I relate an incident from a recent tango workshop: "There was a young Argentine dance instructor in Edmonton. The typical macho male profile. Sexualized everything. At one point his dance partner added an unsolicited comment and he grabbed her by the throat, lightly, and said jokingly, 'The only time I want to hear from a woman is when she is moaning on her back.'"

"OK. So you want to avoid that version of masculinity. And not just because it is abusive, but because it is weak. Real strength comes when you combine the masculine and the feminine. It gives you a range of expression and response. You can adapt to each situation and be soft and sensitive when appropriate or strong and defiant when required. But it is that flexibility and range and the wisdom to know what best fits a situation that gives you real power. You are not an abusive man. You carry a lot of personal power through your day-to-day life as well as onto the dance floor."

I mull that over.

She continues, "But secondly, give the woman some credit. We can take care of ourselves. It takes a woman about three seconds to determine whether she can trust the man. If she doesn't, she leaves the dance floor. Simple." She adds generously, "I want you to know that I would gladly dance with you anytime, anywhere."

"Thank you." I soak up the affirmation.

Gwen pulls me back to the lesson. "Tango pushes those buttons of trust, intimacy, and communication. That's why we love it. But dancing is not about reliving old patterns. You are a virile man dancing with an independently-minded mature woman. This is your opportunity to undo those patterns and act in an unscripted, empowering way, the chance to step off this wounded child treadmill."

Enough already with sexual abuse trauma continually showing up where I least need it. Time to open up to strength, power, presence. Shred the script: closeness does not hurt; sensitivity is not weakness.

"Let's dance again," Gwen suggests. She puts on a slower, moody piece, my preferred style, that allows for pauses and swoops and tempo changes. As we enter into embrace she interrupts with one more instruction. "Breathe in deeply."

I cough.

"Breathe," she insists. I comply and she breathes along with me.

"Can you feel the connection, how our bodies are lifting and falling as if in one breath? This is the best way to get that intimate connection, sharing this breath together and feeling each other's chest movement and heart beat."

My eyes well with tears. No one has ever invited me to breathe with the music while holding my partner. I breathe again, less constricted. We move back into the embrace. My right arm wraps around but my hand does not press. She tucks her head in against mine. We share a breath then sway briefly to synchronize our bodies' movements. I take in a second deep breath and we step to the side in a *salido*.

The piece is swelling, changing, shifting, fast and slow, dreamy, direct, soft – three timeless magical minutes accompanied by muses and spirits that are drawn irresistibly to motion and passion. We share one last breath and then the release.

Gwen gives me an extra squeeze. "Beautiful," she says. Lesson learned.

NAME CHANGE

*Jacob was left alone. And an angel wrestled with him until the breaking
of the day. When the angel saw that he did not prevail against Jacob,
he touched his hip socket, and Jacob's hip was put out of joint as he
wrestled with him. Then the angel said, "Let me go, for the day has
broken." But Jacob said, "I will not let you go unless you bless me."
And the angel said to him, "What is your name?" And he said, "Jacob."
Then he said, "Your name shall no longer be called Jacob, but Israel,
for you have striven with God and with men, and have prevailed.*

Genesis 32:24-32

The ceiling pulsates as I lay in bed, mulling over a question that has
been troubling me since the dream about the orphanage. Who was
that unnamed child? Who am I? A clean start and a new identity
need a new name. Am I no longer Fred Kruk?

My hip continues to throb as I wrestle with this dilemma.
Why is that familiar? The Bible story of Jacob surfaces, in which he
wrestles with God until he gets a new name, and a sore hip out of
the deal! That was what I had been doing these past 50 odd years:
wrestling with God, extricating myself from underneath the shame
and wounding that had been dumped on me as my birthright in an
attempt to reclaim dignity and cleanliness of soul. And I had prevailed! Not only have I earned a name change, there was a Biblical
precedent for changing it.

This *renaming* necessitates a summoning of *mis tres amigos*, as
they are implicated in this transition. My ego had been functioning in a fairly integrated fashion lately, so it had been a time since
we had had a conference, and they were slow to materialize in my
consciousness.

They approach with reticence, no doubt sensing something

sinister about our get-together. Foxy skulks low to the ground, tail dragging. Raven hip-hops, herky-jerky, head tossing side to side. Monkey seems exceptionally awkward, his legs too long for a relaxed gait. With nothing to swing from, he keeps falling over himself. They eventually all settle down in front, motionless.

"Well, I guess you are wondering why I called this meeting," I say, attempting to deflect with a cliché the awkwardness of our encounter.

"It has been awhile," Raven responds with obvious indignation. He has difficulty imagining how I could have managed so long without his guidance. "I presume it is not because you want our counsel?" his voice rising slightly, betraying a hint of curiosity.

I swallow and turn my eyes away. How to sugar-coat my intentions? Foxy is now curled up with his tail shielding his eyes. It flicks nervously, just enough to allow him to monitor my intention. Monkey is attempting to sit on his haunches but keeps falling off sideways.

"I am getting a new name," I say. A stillness follows, allowing for my words to sink in.

Raven ruffles his feathers. "So Kruk doesn't suit you anymore," he snaps.

"That's sort of it," I mutter. "I mean, Kruk is fine, I just want to create some space for my matriarchal lineage. Maybe if we could blend my Celtic and Ukrainian heritage somehow."

"You could be a Cuke," suggests Monkey, more out of a lame attempt to be helpful than witty. I laugh respectfully. Raven doesn't.

"OK. So what's the deal," Raven confronts me.

"I am looking for a new image. I need to start fresh. Unload all the baggage," I offer, somewhat apologetically.

Raven stands defiant, not responding.

"Nothing personal," I continue, "but my family history is just so loaded with crap. I don't need to carry that energetic connection anymore. There is that other business, too," I continue. "No fault of yours, Foxy," gathering the courage to address him directly, "but your namesake was a pervert. I don't need to carry that energetic connection anymore. Fred has got to go."

"Now back off a minute," croaks Raven. "You get a notion and you think everyone else has to fall in line. Changing a name is one thing. Thinking you can ditch your past or that you won't need guidance in the future is more than a little presumptuous."

I make a quick retreat. "Okay. What do you propose I do?"

"Let's get honest here. Quite frankly, we have all been feeling a little constricted the last while. A few changes could be just what are needed. Why don't we put our heads together and come up with some new *shtick* that keeps us all in the game but playing on the same side."

That prospect had never occurred to me, but it certainly had its appeal. My mind was swimming, too distressed to really make a clear assessment of the situation.

"So what's the game?" I ask.

MONKEY'S IDEA

You do not have to be good.
You do not have to walk on your knees
for a hundred miles through the desert, repenting.
You have only to let the soft animal of your body love what it loves.

Mary Oliver, *New and Selected Poems*

"I've got an idea," interjects Monkey. He had been out of the centre of attention for the past while and his unexpected pronouncement rouses me from my fog. I greet it with reticence. Monkey has had ideas before, of course, lots of them, but none of them good. Bizarre images of past Monkey-incited antics flooded my mind. On any other occasion his offer would have been dismissed, but in this circumstance I am desperate. We all are. "We could go somewhere, do something." He is now becoming animated and eagerly looking for something to swing from.

"Anywhere in particular?" I ask.

"Umm, Argentina."

"What on earth for?" the three of us chime in unison.

"To dance tango," Monkey responds matter-of-factly, as if it should be self-evident.

The image of Monkey dancing tango is so hilarious that it lifts my dejection. "Monkey, I have never danced in my life, and you would be the reason. That is all I need, to have you swinging and groping your way around the dance floor."

"Off to Argentina to dance tango," responds Raven, adjusting his stance. "It has possibilities," he says, pensively. He is as surprised to say it as the rest of us are to hear it. "I think it would be the perfect venue for getting you out of a rut, onto a new track and practicing some of this learning that you have been through. And there would be something for everyone. Monkey could get his jollies. Foxy could obsess about keeping him in line and I would get to see the bigger picture.

"And what is the bigger picture, dare I ask?"

"Use your imagination. Get into your body. Maybe even add a little fun."

"I could have said that," interrupts Monkey, wanting to make sure that he retains credit for the idea. That Monkey could have said that makes the prospect somehow less attractive. Monkey, with his irrepressible libido, is rigged up like a suicide bomber, ready to go off at any moment.

Raven continues, not pleased with having been interrupted. "Back to the bigger picture. There is the whole redemptive theme about tango: "the light shines in the darkness," that sort of thing." Raven pauses to see if Monkey or Foxy or I are getting his point. We respond with blank stares.

"Tango originated in La Boca, Buenos Aires, the port district of the late 1800s and early1900s, when the air was thick with human degradation and the stench of blood from the slaughter houses, and where the men were many and the women, few, were forced into the sex trade. Tango was born out of the brothels and bordellos of an oppressed citizenry, and look what has come of squalor," says Raven excitedly, as if uncovering clues in a detective mystery. "An entirely new genre of music emerged that embodies the pathos and melancholy and perversity of the setting but weaves in beauty and elegance and hope. That is what makes this dance so magical, almost mystical." He pauses to give us opportunity to catch his enthusiasm. It isn't happening.

"And the fun comes in where?" Monkey asks, bewildered.

"I was hoping for something a little more dignified," I say. The music from the tiny music box on my sister's dresser begins to play in my mind, with the young gallant soldier standing so sure and strong, upright and wooden, holding his delicate ballerina in her white lace and tutus, his courage and virtue embroidered in gold on his epaulettes, turning her round and round, never faltering, nor varying his position – all so safe and sanitary and sanctified. This is the vision that had inspired my quest over the last fifty years: the hope of healing the wounds, erasing the shame, reclaiming my position on the pedestal alongside my ballerina. "Let me back up on the pedestal!" I plead.

Raven is unsympathetic. "The age of innocence is past. You are no longer a child. This is an adult world of complexities and subtleties and intuiting one's way in and out of situations. There are no black and whites, clear-cut rights and wrongs. You don't grow up by avoiding those nuances but by integrating them. One must have the courage and wisdom to venture into the shadows."

True. Much has evolved, shifted, expanded. I am no longer wooden, my virtue as brazen as brass buttons. I am not constant, reliable, and stiff. The dance of life has evolved in complexity. As much as I might desire it, there is no going back to an age of innocence and purity with well-pressed uniforms and white-laced tutus, where women are as lifeless as music-box ballerinas and a man wears his valour and virtue on his sleeve. I have transformed the abusive dynamic of power over into a dance of mutuality and trust.

My mind begins to race. Are there similarities between my process and the origins and development of tango? Despite its steamy sexual overtones, maybe tango could be a resolution rather than a perpetuation of the abusive, misogynist models of sexuality that have undermined my search for intimacy. With proper attention, it could serve as a sort of laboratory to address and resolve the abhorrent socialization and family dysfunction that I internalized as a child. The self-censorship and shame rooted in childhood trauma and reinforced by my dualistic religious training could be routed on the dance floor! All that I need do, according to Raven, is to embrace my shadow.

"Embracing my shadow it is, then," I concede, and turn instinctively to Monkey, offering him my arm.

"Wee-haa!" he hoots, then latches on with one arm and slings the other one over my shoulder. This seems to be a comfortable fit. Better than having him tagging along behind, in trouble and out of sight.

THE DANCE OF LOVE

Dance me to your beauty with a burning violin.
Dance me through the panic till I'm gathered safely in.
Touch me with your naked hand or touch me with your glove.
Dance me to the end of love.

Leonard Cohen, *Dance Me to the End of Love*

Our friends from the Edmonton tango community, Geoff and Susan, world travellers, had assured us that we could get by comfortably in *Buenos Aires* on $20 a day and a *por favor*. Always suckers for a good deal, we packed up our tango shoes and our Spanish-English phrase dictionary and set off on a pilgrimage to the *Mecca* of our new found religion. Twenty-four hours later, only slightly maimed, we hobbled off the plane into the mystical world of dance and romance, thrilled at the prospect of conquering a foreign culture and putting our tango expertise to the test.

Although no longer navigable at $20 per day, BA still remained quite a tourist bargain and we were enthralled with the elaborate architecture, the extravagant European craftsmanship, the plenitude of parks and roads that spread out forever, (one street, 32 lanes!). Getting around should have been easy with taxis outnumbering private vehicles, fares dirt cheap and drivers courteous and honest (although they all drove like *Mario Andretti wannabes*).

The real challenge came in the communication. Our dusty old dictionary was just not up to the task, nor were we. Perhaps we travelled in different circles than our friends, but a *por favor* just would not cut it. Here in *San Telmo*, the heart of tango and a very authentic Argentine neighbourhood, English was as distant as a plate of salad greens in a *parilla* (BBQ spit in the middle of the restaurant – a popular Argentine venue). The little Spanish we knew was apparently from some other continent and bore no familiarity to the street dialect and the distinctive Argentine *Castellano*, which often left us stuck on a street corner, not knowing how to ask directions, or standing stupified in front of a vendor with a line-up behind, haplessly trying to count out an undeciphered amount of change.

It was downhill from there. Before we had left Edmonton, I had made great pains to ensure that I would have email contact with my teens when I was away, so I had purchased a little laptop and brought along the proper power adaptors. One minor miscalculation. In Buenos Aires no one has home email. This is theoretically not a problem because at every street corner there is a telecommunications cafe that has phone service and internet access except that the Spanish keyboard is different and no matter what combination of keys I pressed I could not get the @ key to appear in my email address line. The shop owner apparently couldn't understand my dilemma or didn't care as I sat pathetically staring at a room full of computers and not able to use one of them. I was heartbroken.

Plan two: Call the only people we knew in Argentina who spoke English, our friends in Patagonia whom we were meeting later on in our trip. When I lifted the receiver, instead of a dial tone I got a thirty second taped message of more *Castellano* Spanish. Back to the desk clerk I went with the phone number in hand and asked him to dial. He had no more success than I did. Apparently the phone system was as unnavigable as the internet, even to the locals. (In truth, I don't recall anyone having much more success with the phone system dialing out of region; there seemed to be a complicated series of codes that had to be cracked like the combination on a lock.)

I walked out a broken man, 10,000 miles from home with no way to make contact with anyone I loved or who cared about me. If we were to be mugged by a taxi driver and dropped off the end of a pier, (which we feared was going to happen at one point), no one would be any the wiser.

Off we went in search of a place to regain our composure, perhaps a quiet cafe for a good cup of coffee and some solitude. We were met at the door of a quaint out-of-the-way establishment by an elderly, elegantly dressed woman who greeted us formally in the textbook Spanish - the same Spanish that I had been studying for months prior but to this point had never been able to use. This was a homecoming! Someone whom we understood! The feeling was so overwhelming I walked in, went over into the corner and crumbled into a weeping, convulsing blob. Afraid that my hysteria might be contagious, Patricia and our proper, well-spoken host pulled away into the other room to address the task of ordering some coffee. As it turned out, this was not in fact a coffee shop but rather a *chocolateria*, with coffee merely a chaser for chocolates.

"No, no, we don't want chocolates," Patricia tried to explain, as we had been on a three day diet of meat and cheese, (the only menu item we knew how to order, served everywhere all the time). Her protestations were interpreted as wanting more chocolates and merely incited the woman's eagerness to satisfy us. In desperation Patricia pulled out her dictionary with her spare hand, the other one carefully balancing the saucer of chocolates and coffee, and tried to find some phrases about ordering food. The only phrase she could come up with in our pathetically inadequate phrase dictionary was, "I would like to start with the onion soup, please."

Pitching the dictionary, Patricia committed both hands to managing more chocolates while I slowly recovered from my convulsions in the corner and returned to normalcy. Apparently the emotional release was cathartic and after washing down our sweets with a shot of espresso we were ready to face the day again.

The agenda for that day was to make it to a *milonga* (tango dance). We had thoroughly researched the wheres and whens before we left Edmonton so again, presumably, we were well prepared. Not far from our residence was the *Confiteria Ideal* with the marble floor and pillars that often appear as a foil for the glitz of tango movies. Dressed theatrically in our dancing attire and pesos, maps and brochures in hand, we headed out onto to the street corner to flag down a taxi and direct him to our destination.

Another minor miscalculation. It was Sunday in Buenos Aires: there were huge political protests going on in the city centre. En route to our destination the traffic came to a complete halt. As our driver could take us no further we were asked for the fare and politely instructed to get out. Between us and our destination was a 30 lane highway, a park and a thick mob of protesters. Off we trekked dressed in our tango finery, Patricia balancing precariously in her high-heeled heels, and I in my *Carlos Gardel fedora*, trying to look as inconspicuous as two penguins.

By the time we made it to the *Confiteria* our shoes were muddied, we were exhausted, and our tango luster had thoroughly faded. Patricia, whose feet had been troubling her earlier, now was in no condition to be dancing. We plunked ourselves down at one of the tables and resigned ourselves to being spectators. After a seemingly interminable period of sitting on the sidelines, I determined that I was going to get in on the action. Since my partner was out of commission, this meant I was going to have to ply my trade on the open market and wade into the sea of experienced local dancers.

Tango etiquette, which I had properly researched, included numerous cultural anachronisms, all seemingly designed to protect the males inflated but fragile ego. One such customs was, if you wanted to dance with someone, you eyed her from across the room. If she reciprocated with eye contact it indicated that she was interested in your offer. In this discrete manner, a woman would gracefully accept or rebut a man's offer without anyone else being any the wiser. The problem was that, without my glasses, I could barely determine the sex of a person from across the room, let alone whether she (or he) was returning eye contact.

I did exactly what any culturally insensitive, boorish Canadian would do in that circumstance. I brashly paraded down the sidelines and started propositioning the women who weren't dancing. I was not one of those machismo Argentine *tangeros* who could not deal with rejection. I took blow after blow directly to the ego but continued to proceed down this line until, at the very end, an elderly woman with pink hair took pity on me.

Up we went on to the floor. After only a few steps into the dance this poor maligned woman began screaming at me, in Spanish of course. I had no clue what she was upset about and began vehemently defending myself in English, of which she couldn't understood a word. I became desperate. My training in *tangero* folklore had made clear that if a woman walked out on you in the middle of a dance, I as a proper *tangero*, totally humiliated, would have to go out back and stab myself. (All tango violence is knife inflicted. They like their knives more than their lives.) So in the middle of the dance, in the centre of the dance floor we are squared off, she infuriated, I desperately pleading as if for my life. Fortunately she stuck the dance out and I lived to tell. Returning to the table devastated, Patricia attempted to console me, "At least you had the nerve to try."

OK. Now we are at a serious impasse. I could accept the language barrier and that we could not be understood well enough to order a proper coffee without chocolates or something other than a plate of meat and cheese, but to not be understood on the dance floor with the universal language of dance was too much for me to come to terms with. Something was seriously askew. We needed help.

The next day our agenda was adjusted to include more tango

lessons. Our host was also, conveniently, a dance instructor, so we booked a session. We showed her our stuff, fitting in all the kicks and pivots and spins we could manage, then stopped to accept praise.

Her muted compliment, "Well you sure know a lot of steps." Another *but*. "But you are lacking in an energy connection." She then wafted into an esoteric explanation about how we were to envision this ball of light between us which would guide and empower the dance. Patricia got all excited as this energy stuff apparently makes perfect sense to her. For me it was more confusing that the pink-haired lady screaming Spanish to me in the middle of the dance floor. *See the energy, feel the energy.* I come up short again. Apparently all that learning, all those lessons, amounted to nothing because I could not get the energetic connection. I was back on the dance floor at *La Boheme* desperately trying to be *right here and not in front of myself or behind myself.*

I start pulling threads together. Breathing, sensing the energy, leading with the chest, they all orbit around the heart chakra. I had been doing my classic disconnect, splitting my physicality into what happens from the waist down and the neck up and leaving the heart out of it altogether. According to this teacher, and contrary to the tango folklore, tango is not about studly men and slutty women doing sultry, seductive steps. It is all about the heart, the key element that I have been understandably, quite reluctant to embrace. Tango is a dance of love.

Am I up for this? Certainly love factors heavily into Patricia's and my dance experience, (as it does with most everything we engage in). But to unabashedly parade my affections out onto the dance floor to share it indiscriminately with whomever my dance partner happens to be?

This question follows me deep into the night. As I drift into the *Land of Nod* familiar voices started up in conversation.

Monkey is first to weigh in. "Well this certainly was a dud.

One dance with a pink-haired lady and you are swearing off sensuality altogether. I thought we were headed into the cesspool of illicit love. You come out a eunuch. We might as well have stayed in the church."

Foxy of course, objects, although the invitation to return to the church has its appeal. "Haven't you heard anything. He's ranting about love on the dance floor. I knew it would come to this!"

"Give your heads a shake, both of you," chimes in Raven, self-appointed arbiter and presumed voice of reason. "You are both missing the point. This is no longer about *big head verses little head, super-ego verses id*. Stop battling and surrender to the seat of wisdom, the heart."

"No fun for me. I am out of here," asserts Monkey.

"This whole experience has been definitely underwhelming," adds Foxy. For the first time - and likely last - the two of them are in agreement. "I'm coming with you," Foxy calls out to Monkey. Off they walk together, arm in arm.

Raven watches with bemusement. "I think, overall, that is a fairly appropriate resolution of the situation." Then he too fades into the misty recesses of dreamland.

STILL POINT

The 10,000 kilometer flight home from Buenos Aires provided time and space to recover from the humiliation and frustration of enduring three weeks as a *gringo*, a genuine foreigner but an imposter in every other way, a misfit, a cartoon in someone else's movie. I am not Argentine. I am not a *tangero*. I don't embody the machismo and bravado of the Latino (nor do I care to). I do not sweep my partner off her feet and into my arms and boldly parade her around the dance floor with flair and *panache*. (I was lucky to escape the dance floor with my life, let alone my dignity.)

I am at a crossroads, at the point of dropping the dream altogether or infusing it with a new vision. The initial charge, the thrill of snuggling in with a pretty lady, the ego satisfaction of doing some fancy steps without falling or kicking someone, the mystique of an exotic dance in a dimly lit cafe, have all faded. The body issues internalized from my childhood abuse have for the most part healed. In fact, if I had not been in the habit of journaling, I would likely by now have forgotten about them altogether. In short, all the sparring of Foxy and Monkey, the juice that brought me onto the floor in the first place, the enchantment that captured Patricia and me when we walked down the stairway at *La Boheme* on our *lovers' tryst*, are past.

But still I dance, even though age and ailments have severely curtailed my time on the dance floor. What is it that still draws?

Is there is something unfinished, something yet to be explored or discovered or healed?

On arriving home I am welcomed by an article written by a long-time tango friend, Mary Anne, who shares from her unpublished manuscript some intimate reflections:

> I realized something sacramental about embracing a stranger with love and appreciation, about listening and attending to how the music will be expressed. It is a creative act, each step new in a physical conversation that links not only the present community of dancers, but also the past generosity of composers and musicians. Two dancers join each other, join the community on the dance floor, and join the orchestras in creative expression. Embracing the other, and connecting across time and culture ...

My heart starts thumping. Strains from that ornate pink music box from my childhood begin to resonate. The pedestal beckons. Perhaps there will always be the call to step up, to stand alone with my lover, arm in arm, responsive to no one or nothing else other than the specialness of the shared moment, the connection, the embrace, the dance.

ACKNOWLEDGEMENTS

My gratitude extends to the many resplendent dance partners who have assisted me in this writing. Patricia, my beloved wife of fifteen years, my partner in life as well as in tango, provided continual encouragement to tell my story with dignity and respect. My family, mother and sister in particular, have supported my chronicling of these sensitive pieces of our shared history, acknowledging this as an important piece of my healing.

Then there are the numerous teachers, therapists and mentors who have guided me along this path, most especially of course, Gwendolyn Jansma. Also thanks to my editors, Susan Beech and Christine Mowat, Thanks as well to Jannie Edwards and Jocelyn Brown who provided very valuable feedback and encouragement through their capacity as *writers in residence.*

Most importantly, there are the participants in the story. Special thanks to two childhood friends, Scott and Sandy, critical to this story, who resurfaced serendipitously at the time of this writing. I have attempted to record everyone's involvement fairly and with compassion. This story waited to be written until I was able to embrace everything with love. As twenty, thirty, forty years have transpired over the course of this journey, my memory may have waned somewhat. However, I am convinced that over that time my heart has trued.

ABOUT THE AUTHOR

Aydan Dunnigan received a Master of Divinity Degree from Lutheran Theological Seminary, Saskatoon. Formerly an ordained pastor of the Lutheran Church, Aydan now works with adults with disabilities for Alberta Social Services. Aydan is a recent winner of a writing competition focusing on earth-based spirituality.

Aydan and Patricia Dunnigan keep their heritage home in Edmonton open to the comings and goings of eight adult children and sixteen grandchildren. Patricia keeps her finger in her consulting and counselling career. Both continue to explore evolving therapies for treatment of trauma. In addition to tango, they enjoy writing, hiking, skiing, photography, and most other outdoor activities.